The Taxobook

Principles and Practices of Building Taxonomies

Part 2 of a 3-Part Series

Synthesis Lectures on Information Concepts, Retrieval, and Services

Editor
Gary Marchionini, *University of North Carolina, Chapel Hill*

Synthesis Lectures on Information Concepts, Retrieval, and Services is edited by Gary Marchionini of the University of North Carolina. The series will publish 50- to 100-page publications on topics pertaining to information science and applications of technology to information discovery, production, distribution, and management. The scope will largely follow the purview of premier information and computer science conferences, such as ASIST, ACM SIGIR, ACM/IEEE JCDL, and ACM CIKM. Potential topics include, but not are limited to: data models, indexing theory and algorithms, classification, information architecture, information economics, privacy and identity, scholarly communication, bibliometrics and webometrics, personal information management, human information behavior, digital libraries, archives and preservation, cultural informatics, information retrieval evaluation, data fusion, relevance feedback, recommendation systems, question answering, natural language processing for retrieval, text summarization, multimedia retrieval, multilingual retrieval, and exploratory search.

Automated Metadata in Multimedia Information Systems: Creation, Refinement, Use in Surrogates, and Evaluation

Michael G. Christel

2009

The Taxobook: Principles and Practices of Building Taxonomies
Part 2 of a 3-Part Series
Marjorie M.K. Hlava

ISBN: 978-3-031-01160-3 print
ISBN: 978-3-031-02288-3 ebook

DOI 10.1007/978-3-031-02288-3

A Publication in the Springer series
SYNTHESIS LECTURES ON INFORMATION CONCEPTS, RETRIEVAL, AND SERVICES #36

Series Editor: Gary Marchionini, University of North Carolina, Chapel Hill

Series ISSN 1947-945X Print   1947-9468 Electronic

The Taxobook

Principles and Practices of Building Taxonomies

Part 2 of a 3-Part Series

Marjorie M.K. Hlava

Access Innovations, Inc., Albuquerque, New Mexico

SYNTHESIS LECTURES ON INFORMATION CONCEPTS, RETRIEVAL, AND SERVICES #36

ABSTRACT

This book outlines the basic principles of creation and maintenance of taxonomies and thesauri. It also provides step by step instructions for building a taxonomy or thesaurus and discusses the various ways to get started on a taxonomy construction project.

Often, the first step is to get management and budgetary approval, so I start this book with a discussion of reasons to embark on the taxonomy journey. From there I move on to a discussion of metadata and how taxonomies and metadata are related, and then consider how, where, and why taxonomies are used.

Information architecture has its cornerstone in taxonomies and metadata. While a good discussion of information architecture is beyond the scope of this work, I do provide a brief discussion of the interrelationships among taxonomies, metadata, and information architecture.

Moving on to the central focus of this book, I introduce the basics of taxonomies, including a definition of vocabulary control and why it is so important, how indexing and tagging relate to taxonomies, a few of the types of tagging, and a definition and discussion of post- and pre-coordinate indexing. After that I present the concept of a hierarchical structure for vocabularies and discuss the differences among various kinds of controlled vocabularies, such as taxonomies, thesauri, authority files, and ontologies.

Once you have a green light for your project, what is the next step? Here I present a few options for the first phase of taxonomy construction and then a more detailed discussion of metadata and markup languages. I believe that it is important to understand the markup languages (SGML and XML specifically, and HTML to a lesser extent) in relation to information structure, and how taxonomies and metadata feed into that structure. After that, I present the steps required to build a taxonomy, from defining the focus, collecting and organizing terms, analyzing your vocabulary for even coverage over subject areas, filling in gaps, creating relationships between terms, and applying those terms to your content. Here I offer a cautionary note: don't believe that your taxonomy is "done!" Regular, scheduled maintenance is an important—critical, really—component of taxonomy construction projects.

After you've worked through the steps in this book, you will be ready to move on to integrating your taxonomy into the workflow of your organization. This is covered in Book 3 of this series.

KEYWORDS

taxonomy, thesaurus, controlled vocabulary, search, retrieval, ontology, knowledge organization, classification, theory of knowledge, metadata

Contents

This book is dedicated to all taxonomists, past, present, and future. My team at Access Innovations worked hard and long to bring this book to fruition. It would not have been done without their encouragement, patience, and support.

List of Figures

Preface

Most of us are keenly—personally—aware that over the past several years, information on the Internet has been rapidly expanding, with a flood of information pouring out of computer screens to people everywhere. In 1998, Google reported 3.6 million searches for the year. In 2012, they reported an average of over five billion searches *every day*. That's an increase of over 52 million percent! They claim 67% of the search market, so there remains another 33% of the market of searches to add to that five billion.

We use search often. We use search so often that "Google" has become a verb, at least in practice. "Google it" has become an everyday phrase. Early in my career, searching the Internet (or its precursor, DARPAnet) was the purview of professionals with special training, special access, and special equipment. We were an elite group of gatekeepers, in a way, with access to a corpus of knowledge desirable to researchers but inaccessible except through professional searchers.

In response to our search queries—when we "just Google" something—the search engines like Google, Yahoo, Ask, and others return millions of hits within milliseconds, but how many of those millions of hits does the searcher actually need… or want? How often do you find that the site you seek is at the top of the search results page? How often do you find that the search results don't include what you seek, or that it is buried ten pages down? How often do you look through ten pages of search results to see if your desired site is listed at all? How do we contend with this exploding flood of information and find what we actually need? Search needs help!

A parallel expansion—or explosion—has been occurring in intranets, where individual organizational and enterprise information resides. Organizations are eagerly adopting technologies that can locate and sort out the information that is wanted and needed. In this environment, as Jean Graef of the Montague Institute put it shortly after the turn of the millennium, "Taxonomies have recently emerged from the quiet backwaters of biology, book indexing, and library science into the corporate limelight." Corporate librarians, information technology specialists, and others involved in information storage and retrieval recognize and acknowledge the value of taxonomies. However, these people often lack an understanding of taxonomies and of how they are created, maintained, and implemented.

In response, we have developed this guide to taxonomy creation, development, maintenance, and implementation. We will progress rapidly from theory to practice because both are critical for a comprehensive knowledge. The guide is intended to cover the full spectrum from the original scoping of the work through its use in tagging (indexing with keywords from the taxonomy), website navigation, search, author and affiliation/organization disambiguation, identification of peer reviewers, recommendation systems, data mashups, and a myriad of other applications.

In Book 1 of this three-part series, I introduce the very foundations of classification, starting with the ancient Greek philosophers Plato and Aristotle, as well as Theophrastus and the Roman Pliny the Elder. They were first in a line of distinguished philosophers and other thinkers to ponder the organization of the world around them and attempt to apply a structure to that world. I continue by discussing the works and theories of several other philosophers from medieval and Renaissance times, all the way through to notable modern library science figures, including Saints Aquinas and Augustine, William of Occam, Andrea Cesalpino, Carl Linnaeus, Rene Descartes, John Locke, Immanuel Kant, James Frederick Ferrier, Charles Ammi Cutter, and Melvil Dewey. Part 8 covers the contributions of Shiyali Ramamrita Ranganathan, who is considered by many to be the "father of modern library science." He created the concept of faceted vocabularies, which are widely used—even if they are not well understood—on many e-commerce websites.

I believe that it is important to understand the history of knowledge organization and the differing viewpoints of various philosophers—even if that understanding is only that the differing viewpoints simply exist. Knowing the differing viewpoints will help answer one fundamental question: *why* do we want to build taxonomies?

With that understanding the process will go much faster. Taxonomists must think in a different way from the normal subject matter expert way of thinking. Taxonomy thinking is thinking in interconnected outlines. It is not the strictly linear thinking shown in a single taxonomy or hierarchical view of a taxonomy—that list with its increasing levels of specificity, but rather thinking for many people taking many approaches to a subject. Those who can sit in an ivory tower and pursue a single thread of thought to eventually developing a full outline of knowledge from their point of view will only sever their single point of view. They will have converts to their way of thinking, but they will not support an interconnected search world with each individual looking in from their own unique perspective. But you know how that works from the first volume, so let's really get to the hands-on work.

In Book 2, I suggest reasons for creating a taxonomy and how it can be used to advantage in an organization. I present and describe various forms of controlled vocabularies, including taxonomies, thesauri, and ontologies, and include methods for constructing taxonomies—or other kinds of controlled vocabularies. Standards, especially information standards, are near and dear to my heart, and I have served on several committees and review boards for many of the information standards published by NISO and other standards-forming organizations. Therefore, Chapter 7 of Book 2 provides an abbreviated list of the specific standards that I feel are most important to knowledge and information professionals, brief descriptions of some of the standards-forming organizations, and the process that they go through in creating these standards or guidelines. While standards might sound like a dry subject best used to cure insomnia, I suggest that they will provide you with an excellent framework for your taxonomy construction project.

Book 3 covers putting your taxonomy into use. It's all well and good to create a beautiful taxonomy that classifies The World as We Know It, that conforms to all of the appropriate standards, and is practically perfect in every way, but what good does it do? In order to get back your investment, you have to integrate your taxonomy into whatever workflow or system your organization employs. In Book 3 we discuss the various ways in which you can apply, implement, and integrate your taxonomy into that workflow, with an emphasis on integrating a taxonomy into search. Lastly, I ponder the future of knowledge management. I don't know exactly where we are going, but I have some good guesses based on where we have been and the trends I see in requests from my clients. Based on my guesses, I provide a few suggestions about areas in which you might start to prepare.

While I can't truly predict the future, I am quite certain that the volume of information coming at us isn't going to go away, lessen in intensity, or slow down. The information explosion is going to continue, and we all need to find ways to make sense of it—to improve retrieval, to refine analysis, to pull out the real value of information so that the people who need it, get it.

I hope that you will find this series practical and useful, and perhaps these volumes will become part of your desktop reference collection. Throughout this series, I attempt to include information that will help you to make a business case for your taxonomy construction project, as well as simple to use, step-by-step instructions for creating a taxonomy and leveraging it in multiple ways throughout your organization.

Acknowledgments

The series started as a series of talks and lectures given to various groups as full-day workshops on how to build and implement thesauri, controlled vocabularies, and databases. The audiences helped hone the messages and poked holes in my assertions when appropriate. This was combined with over 600 engagements over the years with fascinating clients who each needed a similar endpoint but with a unique twist because of their content and their individual visions. These combined with the need to educate staff members in how the work is done and the need to formulate best practices, as well as broad support on the standards bodies, to create an unusual degree of perspective on the knowledge organization and distribution process.

This work would not be possible without the tireless efforts and uncompromising support of many, many people. My business partner and friend for most of my professional life, Jay Ven Eman, has been unstinting in his support and encouragement, although he does occasionally roll his eyes at some of my ideas. The team at Access Innovations, all of whom reviewed the drafts and, in particular, Heather Kotula, Barbara Gilles, Tim Soholt, and David (Win) Hansen,who massaged the drafts, untangled my prose, improved the images and examples, and offered very pertinent suggestions to create the final product. Our customers for providing the content and allowing us to work with it have provided an unparalleled laboratory of material for organization to meet their individual needs. To my own family for their cheerful understanding and putting up with the demands of career and writing, my husband Paul Hlava, my daughters Heather and Holly and their families. And to my mom, Mary Kimmel, who showed me that you can have a career and a happy family too.

Many people encouraged me to write down what I was teaching, and I am grateful for their continued insistence. Tim Lamkins for his early review and insightful comments, clients whose works we reference in case studies and examples, and my industry mentors including Roger Summit, Eugene Garfield, Buzzy Basch, Tom Hogan, and Kate Noerr.

To all of these and more I thank you; I could not have done this without you!
Marjorie M.K. Hlava

CHAPTER 1

Building a Case for Building a Taxonomy

As we discussed in Book 1 of this three-part series, philosophers and great thinkers through the ages have pondered the question of knowledge and information and how it can—or should—be organized. All information can be organized in different ways, according to different perspectives. For our purposes, the way that information is collected, tagged, and presented is the way you want your users or readers to think about it—or, looking at it from another viewpoint, you should collect, tag, and present information the way that your readers or users already do think about that information. I will say this many times throughout this book: Use what the users use.

Leaping forward to the current century, to a modern example, let's think about what you like in the grocery store or other store where you shop most often. You, the user (or the customer), tend to get used to the organization of that store. The store displays items for sale in places you have come to expect. When you arrive at the store, perhaps with your list in hand, you already know which way to turn to get to the department where the items on your list are displayed. There is a familiarity that gives you, on some level, a sense of comfort in shopping there. But when the store reorganizes, is the new layout something you can easily understand? How do you feel, and what happens to your comfort level, if they reorganize and decide to separate the food depending on whether it is organic or conventional, instead of whether it is a dry grain or a juice or a meat? After my local Walmart redid the store floor plan last year, I could not find a thing! Where in the devil did they put the paraffin wax? I thought it might be with canning or with the household cleaners, but, no, it is now located with the Dr. Scholl's foot products near the pharmacy! Why are the pet options all split up? Pet food is together—except for bird food, which was moved to the gardening and outdoor section. A store designer somewhere in the Walmart organization probably thought it made perfect sense, but to me the de-organization was so frustrating that I stopped shopping there for a while.

Do you have the same kinds of frustrations? Then think of your users. Is information presented in a comfortable way for them? Are you using your thought path or theirs? Are those thought patterns the same, or are they vastly different? The best solution for the customers will be to arrange the data as they think of it. That may not be how it is stored in the warehouse, how it is shipped, or how SIC or NAICS or some other industry classification system organizes it. That doesn't really matter. To help your users find the information they need, use the methods and thought patterns your users use. Later in this book, we discuss the techniques of discerning users' thought patterns, which are often discoverable through observation or even aggregated electronically by means of search engine log records.

1.1   TAXONOMIES AND METADATA

What are taxonomies good for? In a word: metadata. Yes, there are other reasons as well, but here let's just cover how taxonomies and metadata are related.

Roughly speaking, metadata is data about data. When you apply the taxonomy, you are using metadata to describe an object, in our industry usually textual information content, although it could be any object, digital or otherwise. The taxonomy term (or other metadata item) is not the information itself; it is only a description. Metadata could be, for example, all those bibliographic citation pieces—the pieces that we find when we are making a catalog card, bibliography, or reference list. It is the information about something else. It might not be just about an article. It might be about a memo or an email, or it may tie into that content retention schedule for records management. It might be describing something in a museum collection or something on the shelf in inventory at a lumberyard. You might be in the grocery store and look at those metadata signs on the aisles that say "Dairy" or "Snack foods." That's metadata for the grocery store, and it helps you locate what you need. It's truly valuable metadata when they reorganize the store! Let the distinction be clear. Metadata falls within the realm of the container or wrapper, not the actual data or information contents.

A taxonomy provides a way to describe content. It is a source of conceptual descriptions for filling the subject metadata field in database records. When you look at a metadata schema (an outline of definition following standards from the W3C for XML definitions or, for example, the standardized set of fields in a typical library catalog record), regardless of who built it, there is some field or element specified for the description of the concept represented in the item. It might be called the subject, descriptor, keyword, or something else.

Lars Marius Garshol has an insightful explanation of what metadata is:

> Metadata is generally defined as "data about data," which is of course a very broad definition. In computer science this is generally taken to mean information about a set of data in a particular representation, which typically means schema information, administrative information, and so on. However, in content management and information architecture, metadata generally means "information about objects" …, that is, information about a document, an image, a reusable content module, and so on. … In general, metadata is best understood as "any statement about an information resource," regardless of what it is being used for, which metadata vocabulary is being used, and how the metadata is represented. [1]

Taxonomy terms are subject metadata, while a taxonomy itself is metadata. That is data about data. Many information organizers today differentiate between administrative metadata, structural metadata, and descriptive metadata. <u>Administrative metadata</u> provides information to help manage a resource: when and how it was created, file type, and other technical information, and who can access it. Administrative subsets may include *rights management* metadata, which refers to intellectual property rights, and *preservation* metadata, which contains information needed to archive and preserve a resource. <u>Structural metadata</u> may indicate how compound objects are assembled, for example, how pages are ordered to form chapters. <u>Descriptive metadata</u> describes a resource or object for purposes such as discovery and identification. This metadata can include elements such as title, abstract, author, and keywords.

Taxonomies are part of a continuum that started as soon as man had too many papers and thoughts to keep track of without some kind of organization. Outlines of knowledge are discussed in Book 1 of this series, but perhaps a passing mention of two particular kinds of organization is quite relevant here. Cataloging and classification, which came to the front of library thinking in the late 1800s, are the precursors to the metadata we talk of today. The classification systems of libraries such as the Dewey Decimal System and the U.S. Library of Congress Classification (LCC) system pioneered by Charles A. Cutter provided a structure for much of the early thesaurus and taxonomy, work. The first thesaurus standards tried to bridge the needs of both communities and paid homage to the style guides they used such as the Anglo-American Cataloguing Rules (AACR and AACR2). Library schools today do not teach or allow as a single elective the cataloging and classification courses, often called technical services courses. They have gathered together a great deal of information offerings from 100 years of research and practice into a single course, which also covers other items having to do with processing books and journals, lasting one short semester. In its place you may find more detail in a metadata course. Some of the richness that made librarians good candidates as taxonomists is lost because they do not have the underpinnings of a good cataloging and classification course and do not yet understand the basics we came from. What the technical services people were doing and what taxonomists do now are akin. They are both subject matter metadata applications. The Library of Congress under Henriette Avram moved into the world of computers in 1964 with the creation of the MARC (Machine-Readable Cataloging) Standard for shared electronic versions of cataloging. One computer could read what other computers had produced using this standard format. It is still widely used today. Some organizations started to gather together this painstakingly cataloged and classified data so that others could share it. This was a very expensive process, often taking a person two hours to build a bibliographic record, containing what we might now call metadata. The biggest proponent of the transition to what we now call metadata has been the Online Computer Library Center (OCLC), which got its start as a shared cataloging resource and made the intellectual jump to metadata, fostering the Dublin Core and the Resource Description Framework (RDF) work we rely on today. As guardians of a huge shared trove of cataloging data, they saw the need to move forward to the broader applications of metadata in the online search world. But I digress; let us return to metadata itself.

Table 1.1: Types of metadata and examples		
Metadata		
Administrative	**Structural**	**Descriptive**
Rights management data	Chapter structure	Title
Preservation data	Page layout	Article abstract
Provenance	Database structure	Indexing keywords
Source		Author information

1.2   HOW ARE TAXONOMIES AND THESAURI USED?

When an organization asks taxonomists to create a taxonomy or thesaurus, it's usually because they want to manage a collection of information resources, such as a database of books, or journals, or journal articles. One of the essential means for managing (organizing) such resources is indexing or categorizing each individual resource (book, journal, or journal article) as a whole, to describe what the resource is about. Abstracts (brief descriptions provided by the author or created by others) are used to serve this purpose. They describe "aboutness."

What is "aboutness?" A good discussion of the epistemological problems mentioned in the following Wikipedia definition is beyond the scope of this work. However, this should provide enough information to move forward in this book:

> "**Aboutness** *is a term used in library and information science (LIS), linguistics, philosophy of language, and philosophy of mind. In LIS, it is often considered synonymous with subject (documents). In philosophy it has been often considered synonymous with intentionality, perhaps since John Searle (1983).*
>
> *R. A. Fairthorne (1969) is credited with coining the exact term "aboutness," which became popular in LIS since the late 1970s, perhaps due to arguments put forward by William John Hutchins (1975, 1977, 1978). Hutchins argued that "aboutness" was to be preferred to "subject" because it removed some epistemological problems. Hjørland (1992, 1997) argued, however, that the same epistemological problems also were present in Hutchins' proposal, why "aboutness" and "subject" should be considered synonymous.*
>
> *While information scientists may well be concerned with the literary aboutness (John Hutchins, 1975, 1977, 1978), philosophers of mind and psychologists with the psychological or intentional aboutness (John Searle, 1983) and language of thought (Jerry Fodor, 1975), and semantic externalists with the external state of affairs (Hilary Putnam, 1975). These seminal perspectives are respectively analogous to Ogden and Richards' literary, psychological, and external contexts (1923), as well as Karl Popper's World 1, 2, and 3 (1977)."* [2]

Taxonomies and thesauri are two examples of controlled vocabularies (see Chapter 3, Getting Started, and the Glossary, for definitions and discussion of "controlled vocabulary"). As such, thesauri are useful for indexing or categorization work involving information resource collections. In controlled vocabularies designed for indexing, each concept covered by the vocabulary is represented by one and only one term that is valid for indexing. (True, a thesaurus contains synonyms, but in most computer-based thesauri, these take the form of "non-preferred" synonyms that point to the preferred terminology for the identification and tagging of the concept. This will be covered in detail in Chapter 4, Terms: The Building Blocks of Taxonomy.)

In addition to indexing, we use thesauri as a way to translate. People often call the same thing by different names in different places throughout the world, as well as in different languages. Although people in the U.S. and in the British Isles all speak English, we speak it differently—we have different terms for the same thing. For instance, a flashlight in the U.S. is called a torch in the U.K. The people of the Indian sub-continent and in Australia speak English, but they each speak a different flavor of English. Even within the U.S., there are regional dialects that can sometimes make understanding one another a challenge! With a common language dividing us, a shared, preferred terminology depending on where we are and who the user group is will go a long way toward mutual understanding and agreement. We need to translate those names into a single way of stating each concept so that we can be consistently understood. To this extent, a thesaurus is a translation system.

We also use a taxonomy or thesaurus for navigation and search, and this is probably the most well-known and widely used function. You are probably using this function every time you go onto the Internet to do something—to find movies and show times at your local theater, to shop for electronics or clothing or books, even to play online games. In addition, people are becoming increasingly clever with ways of using thesauri in search and now for mashups—getting data from many different places and putting it together in different ways [3]. You can put information on a map—and thereby you can track accidents across the country or across a district within a city and use this information to decide where to place additional safety resources, for example—if you've coded the items consistently (consistent coding provides the basis for a variety of new and innovative search implementations. We will cover this concept in detail in Book 3, Chapters 4–6).

Finally, we can use a taxonomy or thesaurus to browse, to drill down to a more granular and narrower layer, to look at a hierarchical list, and navigate down a tree to find information. We may not be sure of our precise endpoint, but a navigable tree offers choices along the way, inviting us to following a path that looks promising. Online retailers often use this function, allowing users to click on categories such as "Kitchen" or "Bath" or "Outdoors," and then to a narrower category such as "Furniture" or "Accents," and so on. The user in this example will follow the tree to narrower and narrower categories until they find the item(s) they are seeking—perhaps a set of bed sheets, or a whirligig for the front yard (in taxonomy parlance we call these "instances," and this is covered in Chapter 4, Terms).

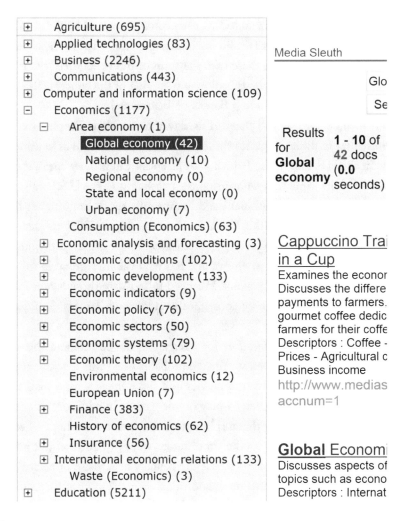

Figure 1.1: Tree navigation.

1.3   WHERE ARE TAXONOMIES AND THESAURI USED?

- In search, to improve search functionality

- In subject browsing

- In the auto-suggestion function in search

- In indexing or categorizing, as subject metadata

- In author subject tagging

- In author submission modules, to indicate author areas of expertise

- In manuscript review modules, for expert reviewer identification

- In member profiles

- In content management systems, such as SharePoint, among many others

- With targeted resources based on subject or user

- In linking to society resources based on the article retrieved

- In filtering data—e.g., spam filters and RSS feeds

- In web crawler applications that automatically search the Internet for content

- In webpage mashups of widgets and such from various sources

- In data visualization

- In social media or on social networking sites

- In mobile intelligence or data mining applications

1.4   FROM LIST TO TAXONOMY TO THESAURUS

People often talk about the many different kinds of vocabularies. Nowadays, "taxonomy" and "thesaurus" often are used interchangeably. Indeed, we can consider a hierarchical thesaurus (which most are these days) to be a fancy taxonomy. In either case, we use the controlled vocabulary for indexing and precise retrieval. The hierarchical array is for our convenience, for either navigating the collection when searching or for organizing the terms.

The differences usually have to do with the structure or lack thereof. Sometimes, taxonomists refer to "flat lists," single-level lists with no hierarchical structure. They can be uncontrolled or controlled lists. An uncontrolled list is a simple, flat structure. Your weekend chore list is an example of an uncontrolled list with no particular formatting. It might look something like this:

- Wash dishes

- Trim bushes

- Clean cat box

- Iron

- Water plants

- Birthday cake

This list uses simple, natural language. It could be a list of candidate terms, serving as an excellent starting point for a taxonomy or thesaurus. But there is no control over semantic ambiguity, no format consistency, and no overall structure. The first time I used this example in a presentation, I asked a new staff member to proofread my slides. But an uncontrolled list is totally uncontrolled. In the course of her review, she tried to add structure to the list by putting "clothes" after "Iron," and "Make" in front of "Birthday cake." Her list would have the structure:

Verb noun (or noun phrase)

Like this:

- Wash dishes

- Trim bushes

- Clean cat box

- Iron clothes

- Water plants

- Make birthday cake

Her version of the list is now controlled, although it is still a flat list.

With a taxonomy, the hierarchy is definitely included. Add related terms, synonyms, and other features as you need them, and you have a thesaurus. At the end of the day, it's the term equivalents that help you most in search, the related terms that will give you a web of knowledge, and the hierarchy that aids in search and browsing.

Taxonomies and thesauri are adjacent on a continuum of vocabulary types, from simple to complex. The continuum starts with flat uncontrolled lists, such as those weekend to-do lists that are not very complex. Name authority files are not very complex. Synonym rings we can constantly add to. After that, we get into the greater vocabulary control provided by taxonomy, thesaurus, and ontology, and finally, we can refine our information into a semantic network.

Normally, an authority list is a flat list, although it can be organized by broad categories. It often defines the "approved" forms of names, with or without the non-preferred synonyms or aliases associated with the preferred form. You have certainly seen authority files in "drop-down" pick lists, like the list of states within the United States that your package can be shipped to when you shop online. As authority files are usually the names of people or places, the builders of these lists provide a finite number of options. For example, places may be geographic locations, like Tacoma, Washington, or an "instance of one" landmark, such as the Golden Gate Bridge or the Washington Monument. If the list has associated variant forms of the names, it can be used to control ambiguity. It also can control ambiguity by providing a consistent form of a name for indexing. If a concept can be called a couch or a sofa or a davenport instead of making the searcher put in all three terms every time they want to search we should allow them to put in the preferred form, say Sofa, and make the other two forms synonyms. In this method we are controlling ambiguity by providing a consistent name for indexing and thereby for search.

Simple lists, such as authority lists, glossaries, gazetteers (a gazetteer is a geographical dictionary or directory used in conjunction with a map or atlas), and dictionaries, are the starting point in complexity. Development into classification and categorization systems comes next, followed by the relationship types that characterize thesauri. Many people start with a taxonomy for categorization and grow into a thesaurus as they identify conceptual relationships and add related terms. Eventually that thesaurus can grow to be an ontology as well. The real benefit is that, as you grow your knowledge organization system from a basic list, each step along the way builds on the previous ones in a continuum. Early work is still a solid foundation as the vocabulary increases in complexity.

1.5   WHY ARE TAXONOMIES AND THESAURI USED?

A short but trite answer would be: "We want to find information." But there is more to it than that. A thesaurus can be used for several different purposes. It is mainly used for **information retrieval**, in one way or another. We use it in information retrieval both on the search end and in the indexing or tagging of the records. We could use it in searching and not indexing or in indexing but not in searching. The possibilities are listed by Jean Aitchison et al. [4]:

- thesaurus used both in indexing and in searching ("The classic thesaurus"),

- thesaurus used in indexing, but not in searching ("The indexing thesaurus"),

- thesaurus used in searching, but not in indexing ("The search thesaurus"), and

- thesaurus used in neither case.

People might intend to use their thesaurus for both indexing and searching, but unintentionally limit the actual usage to just indexing. Too often, people invest in the labor to tag their data, and then put it into a search software application that doesn't support searching the tags. What a wasted effort! It is the search implementation that makes a difference in how that indexing is used. We cover this in detail in Book 3, Chapters 3-6.

In addition to information retrieval, a thesaurus can also be used as **a guide to a field of knowledge or study**. Your thesaurus might be only a simple browseable list, but it can be an outstanding way for someone to discover the various topics within an area, and how they inter-relate. When a user searches on a given taxonomy term, it is possible for your system to provide suggestions about other, related areas, because those terms are linked in the taxonomy. Knowledge discovery, in this way, can be very helpful to researchers in finding additional resources, even those that might seem peripheral but, by virtue of how they have been indexed and how the thesaurus is constructed, are actually closely related.

A thesaurus can be monolingual or multilingual. In multilingual thesauri, a term record ad-dresses the same concept in different languages. This can be useful for **translation** efforts, as well as multilingual indexing and search. As a translation tool, a thesaurus helps the user to find correct terminology and field-specific jargon. For example, someone interested in cave exploration may be unaware that "spelunking" is another term used for this activity within the U.S. and Canada. This recreational activity may be called "potholing" in the U.K. and Ireland. In addition, how many users are aware that "speleology" is the scientific word to describe the study of caves and the cave environment?

When used as knowledge organization systems, thesauri can be used to **influence people's thinking**. After all, by presenting an outline of knowledge for your organization in a thesaurus, you define the relationships and categories of various concepts and express a way of perceiving the total structure and interaction of parts. While my Walmart puts paraffin wax in the gardening and outdoor section, my local grocery store puts it in the aisle with kitchen gadgets. The designers for the two different stores are working to influence my thinking in different ways—one says paraffin wax is for outdoors, while the other maintains that it is an item that belongs in my kitchen.

We have discussed some of the ways we use a taxonomy: the *how*, the *where*, and the *why*. Taxonomies provide another important link in the information management sphere, as well. They can be thought of as the basic building blocks of the emerging discipline and community of practice known as information architecture.

1.6   THE CORNERSTONES OF INFORMATION ARCHITECTURE

Information architecture is a field of study all on its own, worthy of volumes of writings. However, here we provide a brief summary in order to gain an understanding of it as we proceed with our taxonomy project.

In 1976, Richard Saul Wurman (1935–) coined the phrase "information architect" in re-sponse to the large amount of information generated in contemporary society, which is often pre-sented with little care or order. In a speech at the American Institute of Architecture conference in 1976, Wurman said, "I thought the explosion of data needed an architecture, needed a series of systems, needed systemic design, a series of performance criteria to measure it" [5].

The Information Architecture Institue defines information architecture as follows:

1. The structural design of shared information environments.

2. The art and science of organizing and labeling web sites, intranets, online communities and software to support usability and findability.

3. An emerging community of practice focused on bringing principles of design and architecture to the digital landscape.

> Information Architecture Institute, "What is IA?" Retrieved at http://iainstitute.org/en/learn/resources/what_is_ia.php on November 4, 2014.

Taxonomies and metadata are the cornerstones of information architecture. They serve as the foundation for content organization and provide a browseable outline of the content. Taxonomies are the basis for labeling information for storage, for search and precise retrieval, for the labels used on a website, and for site navigation. Taxonomy terms used as subject metadata support 100% recall of relevant information. For people who really cannot afford to miss any of the information in your database, this is a godsend. This is especially true for those who work in patent research, legal research, and medical research. When compliance issues are at stake, there is little room for error in retrieval.

Taxonomies are a grand challenge to your intellectual rigor. Building a hierarchy of terms is an intellectual feat, but applying the taxonomy to data is what really makes the work worthwhile. That is where the rubber hits the road. You have to figure out how to best use those taxonomies. The more ways you can find to use them, the more likelihood they will be supported over your tenure with them. Keeping them current and applying those in innovative, informative ways can create a strong knowledge management platform for an organization. Taxonomies are entirely scalable. Many are finding that taxonomies and thesauri are part of their answer to big data problems and challenges. To make structured information out of unstructured data is part of their purpose.

1.7 SO TELL ME AGAIN: WHY BUILD A TAXONOMY?

I hope that I have convinced you that building a taxonomy or thesaurus is worth the effort, and that all of the work and time you invest will result in wonderful benefits to everyone around you. However, if you need to make a business case in order to sell the idea in your organization, here are some additional points that you can use.

With a taxonomy or thesaurus, which is a structured network of terms, you enable your user's better access to information that includes semantic connections to other terms, and therefore additional related information. Search and retrieval finds useful information by an active search, whereas the semantic connections allow users to discover associated content that they may not have realized existed.

Your taxonomy will guide them to the appropriate terminology, whether this is at the beginning of the information process, as in author submission systems, or at the end, in search and retrieval. Your users and customers will be able to find information faster and more accurately, that is, they will experience better recall and increased precision in their searches.

You have likely heard it said that "time is money" in the business world. By creating a system that allows for faster and more accurate information retrieval, your organization will save money. Users will be more productive because they spend less time finding the right information, and perhaps, by being made aware of conceptually related content, they discover additional information that leads to new inventions, creations, collaborations, and the like.

Your taxonomy project should start with the goal of helping people find useful information, whether by an active search or by discovery through that associated content. A taxonomy provides an organizational structure, a path, that makes it easy to find the way to that desired information. Just as importantly, it describes that structure in a shared language that all users can understand.

In short, the reason to build a taxonomy is to *help people find things*.

This chapter is meant to provide a few points to keep in mind as you begin to think about your taxonomy construction project. I will cover these concepts in much more detail in future chapters.

CHAPTER   2

Taxonomy Basics

The Internet has opened the door to countless website builders and contributors. The result is rapidly accelerating growth, creating a web that is simply too big for people to find what they want reliably. It needs knowledge management.

Beneath the artfully designed graphic interfaces, much of the material on the Internet is actually in the form of databases—collections of data put together in some organized format. The organization of this data yields information, that is, data in meaningful context. There are many different kinds of databases, for example:

- Numeric

- Textual

  ○ Full text

  ○ Bibliographic

- Structured field formatted

  ○ Title

  ○ Author

  ○ Abstract

- Relational

- Object oriented

- Multimedia

These types of databases operate differently. Numeric files are typically not something to which we would apply a taxonomy.

A <u>numeric database</u> is really where computers got their start—processing huge amounts of data in coded form, the U.S. Census data, weather satellite data, or data coming in from the Very Large Array observatory. In fact when Hollerith used his numerical tabulation methods (which led to his development of the Hollerith computer punch cards) to process the U.S. Census starting in 1890, he reduced the time needed to process the data to only three days!

(See https://www.census.gov/history/www/innovations/technology/the_hollerith_tabulator.html.) Such databases are important, complex, and not generally suited to taxonomies.

On the other hand, a taxonomy is suited to textual databases, those that use the full alphabet rather than just numbers and codes for the content display and manipulations, full text or bibliographic. These are the newer form of databases, only coming into widespread conversation in the mid-1960s and full development starting in the early 1970s. Much of this early research work is not computerized and searchable other than in the Google Scholar databases. It is ironic that the information about bibliographic and full text databases is not itself in full text and available. But that is because once it was discovered that the systems worked well, the world began from that point forward to digitize the records. Some organizations are now digitizing back to the beginnings of their journal and bibliographic collections, but most follow the library wisdom of weeding their collections and throwing out the old superseded material. Unfortunately, some of the groundbreaking research is in that older stuff. The work of the COSATI commission headed by Alvin Weinberg is one such set of data that is well worth reading. Some of the things they came up with or discussed are only now beginning to be implemented in the linked data world.

A <u>bibliographic database</u> is the metadata record. It is also much like a library catalog card although it will frequently include an abstract of the full text as well.

A <u>full text database</u> has included all of the written word as a digital record. This usually includes the full articles for example and then the references as well. The publishing community refers to the sections as the "heads" (the metadata record), the "full text" (the body of the article), and the "tails" (the references at the end of the article).

The structure of these databases, with formatted data fields, enables us to apply taxonomies to the information contents of the fields.

Once the data is made into a digital form then the format of the data in the computer becomes important. This includes the way in which the data is laid out on the computer memory itself. The two current major systems are relational database management systems (RDBMS) and object-oriented databases (OODB). The original database management systems (DBMS) are no longer as widely used.

Relational database systems depend on many sets of tables—each stored in a separate place which link to each other using a key file and sub keys—data that is resident in both tables to make the connections. Think of the various columns in the Excel spreadsheet to start, and then add some extra dimensions. The object-oriented database, on the other hand, builds a single record which contains everything related to the object it is describing. The more traditional programming languages, like C+, lend themselves to RDBMS. Newer languages like Java tend toward object-oriented files. The thinking involved is quite different and the syntax to describe each sometimes gets muddled in conversation. You can build an object system with C+; you can build a relational file with Java.

XML (the eXtensible Markup Language) describes an object but is often converted to relational for implementation. Yes—confusing!

Databases increasingly capture multimedia, such as images, videos, and sound. People want to be able to find all of their videos and images, but they often don't use captions. Multimedia data with no text is not well suited to a text-oriented taxonomy. It requires some additional system activities to add verbal descriptions with which taxonomies can be used.

The persistent challenge in databases and on the Internet is finding a way to recognize concepts buried within those collections of information despite an endless variety of author expression. Taxonomies link the original language to shared and readily understood terms.

2.1   VOCABULARY CONTROL AND WHY IT IS IMPORTANT

Vocabulary control is a large part of what we work on in taxonomy and thesaurus development. Vocabulary control is consistently using the same words (in our case, taxonomy terms) for the same concepts. It is important to avoid the duplication of different terms, or expressions, with the same meaning, and the confusion of the same term or expression being used with different meanings (for example, "mouse"—rodent and computer context).

The well-known controlled vocabulary standard ANSI/NISO Z39.19-2010R [6] lists five purposes that controlled vocabularies (including taxonomies and thesauri) serve.

4. **Translation:** Provide a means for converting the natural language of authors, indexers, and users into a vocabulary that can be used for indexing and retrieval.

5. **Consistency:** Promote uniformity in term format and in the assignment of terms.

6. **Indication of relationships:** Indicate semantic relationships among terms.

7. **Label and browse:** Provide consistent and clear hierarchies in a navigation system to help users locate desired content objects.

8. **Retrieval:** Serve as a searching aid in locating content objects.

All of these purposes are directly related to indexing and information retrieval.

Vocabulary control is achieved in a number of ways. First, we control the synonyms—different terms or expressions for the same concept. Synonyms may also be called non-preferred terms. They may also be applied to the "use-for" terms, homographs, or, more commonly in Europe, polysemes.

Homonyms, however, are a different case. These are the words spelled the same way but with different meanings, such as *lead*, which can be used to mean a noun for the chemical element, or the noun, or verb meaning showing the way, directing operations. "Lead" in British English, is the strap or rope or other device that we use to keep physical control of our dog when we take him out for a walk. In nautical terms it is a body of water. In this case as in many others in every language, it leads to puns and jokes, but within a computer search and application to text we need to clearly state the differences. The activity to clearly state the term usage in the same spelling but different meaning is "disambiguation."

We also control the vocabulary by preventing redundancy, managing words and phrases that duplicate the meaning of terms in the taxonomy. By controlling synonyms and duplication, we achieve an important goal for taxonomies: having a single term to represent a single concept.

Vocabulary control is also accomplished through a term's hierarchical position in the taxonomy. This helps to delineate the term's scope of meaning, indicating what it means in a particular thesaurus. Identifying broader and narrower terms and identifying synonyms and related terms further clarify the meaning of the term. For example, the meaning of the term *lead* in a science taxonomy, when it is a narrower term of *Element*, signifies a specific concept to the user just by virtue of its placement. Likewise, the meaning of *lead* as a narrower term of *Management* in a business-related taxonomy represents a specific, but different, concept.

A thesaurus is a controlled vocabulary. Since many thesauri are hierarchical, they may be referred to as taxonomies. However, unlike a simple taxonomy, a thesaurus includes equivalence relationships (synonyms), associative relationships (related terms), and scope notes (we will cover these concepts in Chapter 4, Terms). It may also contain definitions, editorial notes, and mappings from other thesauri and/or from taxonomies.

A thesaurus focuses on concepts, not just the information object, such as a specific document. You can identify the information object or the concept by using the thesaurus. Rather than simply outlining the collection of information objects, as a taxonomy might, a thesaurus serves as a guide to the concepts surrounding those information objects. You can easily see this focus in a multilingual thesaurus term record; it focuses on the concept of the terms, rather than on the term itself in any one language. The focus on concepts is furthered by the inclusion of synonyms and related terms. There are several different ways to display a thesaurus so that you can see the network of conceptual relationships among the terms.

2.1.1   SYNONYMS IN VOCABULARY CONTROL

An important strategy for improving search results is to be sure that everything on a particular topic in the collection can be identified as such, regardless of the words used for the concept. This is where the synonyms in a thesaurus come into play. If we can apply all of the synonyms, we can capture the concept of "couch," whether it is called a couch or sofa, davenport, settee, or multiple seating unit or modular seating. We can gather all of the terms for that concept, including terminology that has changed over time. Capturing synonyms is critical for full retrieval of all materials on a particular topic. This capability might not matter so much in a casual search. However, if you are searching for information for a dissertation, you don't want to discover two years after your publication is issued that someone else had already published on that topic. If you are planning to file a patent, you don't want to find out that the technology is already patented by someone else after you have acquired investment capital and built a whole firm to support your work. In litigation, if you have done your e-discovery and then the other party finds a damning email that your system missed for lack of synonyms, then your system has failed due to vocabulary shortcomings.

Having many different synonyms or non-preferred terms for the same concept is extremely important. These serve as access routes to the preferred taxonomy terms, and therefore to the documents indexed with those terms. My rule of thumb is to have at least 1.5 synonyms for every term in the thesaurus. If you have 500 terms, you should have a minimum of 750 synonyms. This strategy is an important way to build semantic richness into your taxonomy.

We cannot know in advance which term a user will use either in their writing or in their search query. Therefore, allowing many synonyms, including spelling variations, gives powerful access to the data collection the taxonomy is built for.

It may seem redundant to have many terms for the same concept. However, this redundancy will aid your users in retrieving the documents they seek. Each user might search with a different term, but if you include as many of them as you can, and then map them to the appropriate preferred term, you will have a solid system that makes your users happy.

Synonym rings present all synonyms for a concept as equals. For example, a synonym ring might include *descriptor*, keyword, *subject headings*, *thesaurus term*, *taxonomy term*, etc., all meaning roughly the same thing. In a taxonomy, you need to determine which one is the primary usage and make the others synonyms. In a synonym ring, they remain equals, and any of the terms can be used for tagging.

2.1.2   VOCABULARY CONTROL AND KEYWORDS

The word "term" applies to an item in a taxonomy that is a valid descriptor for indexing. "Keyword," according to ANSI/NISO Z39.19-R2010, is a "word occurring in the natural language of a document that is considered significant for indexing and retrieval" [7]. The words an author uses to describe a scholarly paper are "author keywords" and, while they may be significant and meaningful, they are not necessarily chosen from a taxonomy. Keywords may be unique to a document and may or may not be recognized in a controlled vocabulary. A searcher tries to pick significant and meaningful words to retrieve a document, words considered likely to be in the document. For a free text search, this approach may be successful, as long as the document's author used those same exact words (restaurant, eatery, greasy spoon, canteen, bistro, diner, cafeteria, etc.).

2.2   INDEXING AND TAGGING

The primary purpose for a taxonomy or thesaurus is to translate words for concepts in a document into a common set of terms. A taxonomy or thesaurus is also known as an indexing language. Indexing is the process of recognizing concepts in written material and the correspondence of the words with the taxonomy terms, and then assigning the terms to the documents. The translation of concepts to taxonomy terms must be done consistently, so that the same indexing terms are applied for the same concept every time. The stage is then set for accurate information retrieval. With a rich thesaurus indicating semantic relationships among terms, we can suggest conceptual similarities, not only helping people find the document or information they are seeking, but also linking to additional material that may be of interest. The centerpiece of the entire process is the taxonomy as the information management tool and search aid.

Indexing can be described as the systematic application of taxonomy terms to describe what a document is about. ANSI/NISO Z39.19 explains the role of controlled vocabularies in indexing as follows:

> *Indexing is the process of assigning preferred terms or headings to describe the concepts and other metadata associated with a content object. Indexing covers any system or procedure in which the selection and organization of terms requires human intellectual decisions at some point in the process. Computer processing may also be a part of the process for storing and manipulating the terms in a controlled vocabulary or to identify content objects to which certain terms or combinations of terms have been assigned or should be assigned.*

> *The process of indexing, therefore, involves selecting preferred terms from one or more controlled vocabularies or other sources to describe a content object.*

> *The effectiveness of indexing as a means for identifying and retrieving content objects depends upon a well-constructed indexing language. Research in the field of information science has shown that controlled vocabularies improve both precision and recall in searching. For example, they improve precision by defining the scope of terms and they increase recall by retrieving documents that employ different terms for the same concept.* [8]

In another example of loose vocabulary control in the taxonomy domain, the term "tagging" has crept into use as a casual alternative. What we would call a "near-synonym" in taxonomy parlance, "tagging" refers to using a word that isn't exactly a synonym but is close enough to pass within the domain. A non-professional might "tag" a document with a "keyword," while an information professional would "index" the document using the terms of a controlled vocabulary, such as an authority file, taxonomy, or thesaurus. Though both are used to mark the topic of a document or other content item, "tagging" and "keywords" do not imply the same rigor or use of a controlled vocabulary.

2.3   A FEW TYPES OF TAGGING

There are three ways that subject tags, keywords, and indexing terms differ in terms of retrieval support.

1. *Free tagging* is the easiest, least vigorous, and generally least effective form of indexing. With free tagging, any words deemed appropriate can be used to describe a document. One person might tag the document <u>Ideal Dog Foods for Dalmatians</u> under "dogs"; another might tag it with "pet food;" and a third person might tag it with "Dalmatian food;" and yet another simply with the misspelling "Dalmations." Each of these phrases is more or less correct, but to a machine being used to either automatically classify this document or to find it in a search, these phases are all distinct and unrelated. Because the machine is programmed for exact matches, it does not understand the semantic relationships between these concepts; it cannot cluster them together. These tags would return a search result on Dalmatians, but since it is really about food, the result is not helpful at all.

   Two additional issues that arise with free tagging are misspellings and foreign languages. If a tag is misspelled, it is seen as completely different by the computer. Therefore, two articles, one tagged with *Dalmatians* and the other *Dalmations*, would be considered distinct even though they are clearly about the same subject. Only one of these instances would be returned in a search.

   This is also true for foreign languages, even similar ones like British and American English. Variants of the same word (*aluminum* and *aluminium*, for example) are separate listings.

   It would be easy to say that free tagging is therefore useless, but the ease with which it is implemented can be of great assistance. Free tagging is a wonderful way to collect terms from authors, to learn of new conceptual areas and current trends, and to find out what the users and authors think should be in the database (see Chapter 4, Terms, or the Glossary for more about literary, organizational, and user warrant). When dealing with a massive amount of data, speed is important. In this instance, free text tagging can be used for a quick initial pass. For crowdsourced indexing challenges such as Wikipedia, free text tagging can facilitate the layman's attempts to describe a resource by making indexing as simple to complete and accessible as possible.

   If enough people free tag a point of knowledge, they can create a *folksonomy*—a system of classification created through collaborative tagging. The term *folksonomy* was coined by information architect Thomas Vander Wal as a portmanteau of *folk* and *taxonomy*. [9]

2. *Natural term tagging* is a slightly more controlled version of free text in that it uses only words and phrases that appear in the article. While retaining some of the benefit in speed of free text tagging, natural term tagging uses the words in the source text in their natural language as it is spoken or written.

This is the basis of full text search, which relies on an index that includes every word in a document. While the merit of full text search versus a controlled vocabulary search is a continuing debate, the issues with synonyms and foreign languages are still major in natural language tagging.

Using the example from above, if the author of the pet food document uses the spelling *Dalmatian*, a user typing their search query as *Dalmation* will not retrieve this document. Neither would a user searching for *Dalmatian food* if that exact phrase never appears in the article.

3. The last (and arguably the best) option is indexing with a *controlled vocabulary* that corrals and defines the possible indexing terms into one place. In this system, an authoritative body reviews and decides which terms and term phrases are in the "preferred" form and which are not. This group decides which text string, whether a single word or several words together, will best represent the concept to be captured and indexed for later search or display. Ideally, the list will also cluster synonyms, other language forms, and variant spellings (non-preferred terms) under one preferred term. When the terms used for indexing are specified and limited, the problems with free text indexing are solved.

Again using our example document from above, <u>Ideal Pet Food for Dalmatians</u>, when we have a controlled vocabulary that points to *Dalmatians* when our user types their search query as *Dalmations*, this document is retrieved by the user—a desired search result.

Indexing with a controlled vocabulary (a taxonomy or thesaurus) enables high consistency for marking the subject of a document, as well as comprehensive and precise retrieval of information in a document search. The challenge for the taxonomist is specifying an accurate, authoritative list of terms and organizing the terms in a logical way.

2.3.1   POST-COORDINATION VERSUS PRE-COORDINATE INDEXING

Most people think about what they want to search for and type a few words in the search box. By combining words or even taxonomy terms for some concept, the searcher is flexibly coordinating terms at the search stage. It is up to the search software to pull together resources that fit the search query.

In contrast, pre-coordinate indexing is the pre-established combination of terms for highly specific concepts. Here are some examples:

- Automobiles—Motors—Carburetors

- Construction industry—Finance—Law and legislation—Italy

- Genetic engineering—Government policy

- Bunker Hill (Boston, Mass.), Battle of, 1775—Poetry

Pre-coordination of terms is typical of traditional classification systems, such as the Library of Congress Subject Headings [10], the Sears List of Subject Headings [11], or the Dewey Decimal Classification [12], but not of most modern taxonomies and thesauri. Classification systems often concatenate separate concepts into a string of terms. Natural language is not used, but rather a sort of narrowing of the subject as the word strings are put together, as in War—U.S. Civil War—Battles—Battle of Bull Run. When used in indexing, each element of the pre-coordinated term must fit the concept in an information resource exactly.

Pre-coordinate systems were mainly used prior to the advent of computers and are still widely used where a system for searching the contents online is not available. Back-of-the-book indexes are a form of pre-coordinate systems. In the current online environment, very seldom do we put together terms in a pre-coordinate fashion. One of the more difficult challenges in taxonomy development is taking older classified lists and back-of-the-book indexes and making them into a post-coordinate system that is suitable for modern information systems.

In a *post-coordinate system*, a single concept is represented by a single term. Concepts are not combined before use, drawn from a rigid term list, but rather at the time of indexing or of search. The path of post-coordinate terms mirrors what most people do today in the Internet Age. Most searchers type in words as they think of them, usually in the way they would speak them, such as *pet food for Dalmations*. This is called "natural language"; using it in our controlled vocabularies reflects the way users themselves express queries in a search interface. Guidelines for constructing taxonomies and thesauri recommend creating terms using natural language designed for post-coordination. Following this method also supports automated indexing and text mining.

2.4   TAXONOMIES AND HIERARCHICAL STRUCTURE

As previously mentioned, taxonomies are one kind of controlled vocabulary. What distinguishes them from ordinary term lists is the presence of hierarchical relationships, with the conceptually broadest terms at one level (often referred to as the "Top Terms"), "narrower terms" grouped under the top terms, and yet narrower terms similarly grouped under those terms, with the pattern continuing until the most specific terms are reached. In the standard mode of hierarchical display, the narrower terms are underneath and indented to the right of their respective "broader terms":

- Computer equipment

  ○ Printers

  ○ Laser printers

  ○ Inkjet printers

  ○ Dot matrix printers

- Monitors

  ○ Flat screen monitors

  ○ Touch screen monitors

Most of us are familiar with hierarchical structure in document outlines and some tables of contents. We also know them from genus-species relationships in biologic taxonomies or parent-child relationships forming a full genealogy. One example of a taxonomy-like outline is shown below. It's from the Wikipedia article "Outline of knowledge [13]."

Knowledge of humankind

- Humanities

  ○ Classics

  ○ History

    - Language

  ○ Literature

  ○ Performing arts

    - Dance

    - Music

    - Theatre

  ○ Philosophy

- ○ Religion
- ○ Visual arts
  - • Media type
  - • Painting
- • Science
  - ○ Natural Sciences
    - • Astronomy
    - • Biology
    - • Chemistry
    - • Earth Sciences
    - • Physics
  - ○ Social Sciences
    - • Anthropology
    - • Economics
      - - Trade
    - • Education
    - • Geography
    - • Health
    - • Law
      - - Jurisprudence
    - • Linguistics
    - • Political science
    - • Psychology
    - • Sociology
  - ○ Applied sciences
    - • Agricultural science

2.4.1   ANOTHER TAXONOMY EXAMPLE

In the beginning of taxonomy creation it is useful to have a model or at least know what some examples look like. The following is the taxonomy view (terms and hierarchy only) of one main branch of the National Information Center for Educational Media (NICEM) thesaurus. While it is only a branch of the source taxonomy, it constitutes a taxonomy in and of itself. It stands alone, as should all terms and branches within a taxonomy. It displays the standard visual organization of a taxonomy, with more specific terms under and to the right of the broader terms under which they are grouped.

Music

 History of music

 Music appreciation

 Music composition

  Musical arrangement

  Musical notation

 Music styles

  American music

   Country and western music

    Bluegrass music

   Dixieland music

   Zydeco music

 Baroque music

 Big band music

 Children's music

 Choral music

 Classical music

 Dance music

 Flamenco music

 Folk music

 Humorous music

 Impressionism in music

 Instrumental music

  Band music

  Electronic music

  Military music

  Orchestral music

  Piano music

  Solo instrument music

  String instrument music

 Jazz music

 Medieval music

 Modernism in music

 New Age music

 Popular music

 Rap music

 Religious music

  Church music

  Gospel music

 Renaissance music

 Rhythm and blues music

 Rock music

 Romanticism in music

 Vocal music

  A capella music

  Chants

 World music

  African music

  Latin music

 Music theory

  Meter and rhythm

  Musical harmony

 Musical acoustics

 Musical forms

  Concerti

Fugues

Operas

Operettas

Oratorios

Sonatas

Musical suites

Symphonies

Musical groups

    Chamber music groups

    Choirs

    Musical bands

    Musical ensembles

    Orchestras

    Rock music groups

Musical instruments

    Brass musical instruments

        French horns

        Trombones

        Trumpets

        Tubas

    Keyboard instruments

        Accordions

        Harpsichords

        Piano

    Percussion instruments

        Drums

    String instruments

        Banjos

        Cellos

        Double basses

        Guitars

        Harps

        Violas

        Violins

    Woodwind instruments

        Bassoons

        Clarinets

        Flutes

        Oboes

        Saxophones

Musical performances

    Concerts

    Musical conducting

    Solo music performances

Musicology

    Ethnomusicology

What is shown above is only the taxonomy view of a thesaurus. In NICEM, the full taxonomy is implemented as a thesaurus, with each term having a full term record containing all the elements that take a taxonomy to the level of a thesaurus.

Each taxonomy needs to represent the content it is to index. It should be built to be content aware. This taxonomy is designed for the indexing of educational curriculum materials. Sections of it might have some applicability to other information collections, but as a whole it would not be appropriate for a database of journal articles about physics. As we mentioned above, a term in one taxonomy may mean something completely different in another taxonomy. For example, the term *Mercury* would mean one thing in a chemistry thesaurus and something quite different in one about astronomy, or automobiles, or Roman mythology. A taxonomy associated with a database of professional research journals would usually have more specific levels, reaching more deeply to reflect the text of the journals and the details of the science covered.

Shown below is a user interface for a controlled vocabulary. The view on the left side illustrates the hierarchical structure that makes the vocabulary a taxonomy. The term record on the right side shows the extra elements (in the Related Term and Non-Preferred Term fields) that make it a thesaurus.

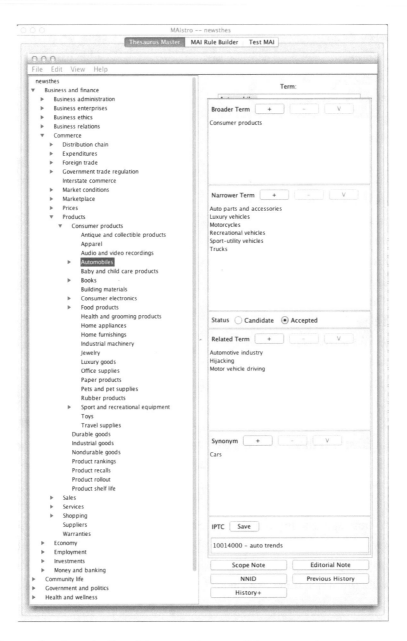

Figure 2.1: Screen shot from the Data Harmony Thesaurus Master main interaction page, taxonomy view on the left, term record view on the right.

2.5   THESAURI: TAXONOMIES WITH EXTRAS

A full-fledged thesaurus has three kinds of relationships. So far, we have just discussed one of them: the hierarchical relationships that also characterize taxonomies. In addition to the hierarchical relationships, thesauri have equivalence relationships and associative relationships.

2.5.1   EQUIVALENCE RELATIONSHIPS

The hallmark of a thesaurus, from Roget's time to the present, has been the presence of synonyms. However, in a thesaurus for indexing and information retrieval, we insist that there be only one term representing each concept that is covered. This dichotomy is handled in a thesaurus through the use of non-preferred terms, which are functionally synonyms. Their corresponding preferred terms are the ones that are intended as indexing terms. The relationship between a preferred term and any of the corresponding non-preferred terms is known as an equivalence relationship. It is also called a preferred/non-preferred term or synonymy relationship (Sofa, Couch, Davenport).

2.5.2   ASSOCIATIVE RELATIONSHIPS

Many concepts are closely related conceptually, but not hierarchically. One is not a broader concept of the other or in the same "family tree," but may well be in an entirely different branch. Such term pairs are often known as *related terms*, usually designated as RT. The relationship is indicated in both term records to show that each is a related term to the other, and alerts the user to consider both terms in indexing or searching. This kind of term relationship is generally referred to as an associative relationship (Nurse RT Nursing, Couch RT Chair).

2.6   AUTHORITY FILES

While we put terms for concepts into a taxonomy, we put the names of people, places, and things into authority lists. Name authority files are the most common kind of authority file. A name authority list captures all the variations on a person's name. For instance, my name might be listed as Marjorie Hlava, or Marge Hlava, or Marjie Hlava, or Margie Hlava, or Marjorie M.K. Hlava, or Marjorie Maxine Kimmel Hlava, or the even longer name I was baptized with. Putting together a name authority file so all variations of a name will point to one "authority" term is increasingly important to ensure that any variation entered by a user will provide accurate and complete search results as social media and online research platforms become more common.

A tremendous amount of effort is being put into name authority files to disambiguate author names. Libraries have long known about the challenges connected to untangling and consolidating author identities, and have created huge name authority files. One of them is the Library of Congress Name Authority File, which contains over 6.5 million names. These kinds of authority files answer the question "Is it Mark Twain or is it Samuel Clemens?" and other similar queries. Not only are there many "pen names" to deal with, but there are also everyday name variations in print and in speech. Name authority files are important to help ensure that we are referencing the correct person and recognizing their works. For example, for authors in the scientific, technical, engineering, and mathematical (or medical) (STEM) realm of publishing, receiving credit for published works and having their works referenced in other publications is an important benchmark. Using my name as an example again, if I were to publish in one of these areas, I would want to ensure that searches all on the variations of my name, including variations with initials like M.M.K. Hlava and Marjorie M.K. Hlava, return every article or publication I have ever authored so that I will be cited correctly in other authors' publications.

There are several large cooperative initiatives in progress to support further name authority work, including ORCID [14], VIVO [15], and VIAF [16]. Each of these assigns an identification number to each author identity, or invites individuals to apply for an identification number to verify their name and be certain that their works are attributed to them appropriately. The process of ensuring that the correct person is identified, the name is in the proper format, and the organizations that he or she is associated with are correctly linked is often called *author disambiguation*. The process of building these large networks may be a social network or a community of like-minded individuals.

Name authority lists are also important in corporations, for product brand names as well as staff names. For example, a pharmaceutical firm researcher may refer to a project by a chemical name, but as the project progresses, its product may be designated by a code, a production name, a special name for clinical trials, and finally a brand name for marketing. In different markets and in different countries, the brand name may be different. This illustrates that the exact same substance will have many different names as it progresses from R&D to production to marketing to being on shelves in a store available for customers to buy. It may then be combined with other substances, repackaged, or have the dosage changed, acquiring additional names in the process. The company needs to keep all of those names together for research, for government regulatory approval, clinical trial tracking, IRS or other tax body compliance, capital asset aggregation, records management tracking, and possibly other purposes. A good authority file supports all of these needs.

2.7   WHAT ABOUT ONTOLOGIES?

Ontology is the newest option in knowledge organization systems (KOSs) [17], and they are attracting a great deal of discussion and research. The purpose of an ontology is to provide a way to connect objects. Just as thesauri can be thought of as taxonomies with extras, ontologies are an even richer version of thesauri. The richness stems from the ability to customize them through additional relationship types, beyond the basic relationships that a thesaurus offers. An ontology can represent complex relationships among objects or concepts themselves.

The word "ontology" has its origins in the efforts of early philosophers to understand and categorize the world around them. It still has that use but has been adopted to apply to terminologies that involve specialized computer-friendly formats, syntaxes, and models, such as those of the Resource Description Framework (RDF) [18], the Web Ontology Language (OWL) [19], and the Simple Knowledge Organization System (SKOS) [20].

The World Wide Web Consortium (W3C) observes,

> *There is no clear division between what is referred to as "vocabularies" and "ontologies." The trend is to use the word "ontology" for more complex, and possibly quite formal collection of terms, whereas "vocabulary" is used when such strict formalism is not necessarily used or only in a very loose sense.* [21]

The formalism referred to by the W3C is the formatting of the resulting file in computer-readable syntax, that is, syntax that computers can interpret and process. Adding to the formalism, ontologies tend to include a set of fairly complex rules governing the relationships.

The main advantage of modern ontologies is that they allow more complexity. An ontology is strong on synonyms, and it supports a swarm of additional relationships. In an ontology, you can establish "is a," "has a," and "is part of" relationships, as well as other kinds of statements that you might want or need in your vocabulary. A couch, for instance, *is a* furniture piece, *has* cushions, and *is part of* a living room set.

The main disadvantage of ontologies is that they're more complex. For indexing, they generally do not provide any advantage over well-developed thesauri. Moreover, the hierarchy (to the extent that one exists) becomes obscured by the variety of associative relationships. It is difficult to develop, let alone use, an ontology that is larger than a few hundred terms. It does have its advantages in some areas, such as pharmacology and genetics, where the focus of research content using an ontology is often the ontology itself, rather than an associated library or database. The ontology becomes the database.

Heather Hedden of Hedden Information Management has wryly commented: "It is an interesting irony that taxonomies, which got their start in biological classification, are now widely used for any form of knowledge, while ontologies, which originally applied to the broad scope of existence, are now used most often in the field of biology" [22].

An ontology may be used mainly to describe a world view or perceived organization of things and/or abstract concepts, and might not be invoked as a formal ontology in a semantic web environment. The authors might have a completely different implementation in mind. Before you get too far into a discussion of ontologies, I recommend that you find out what people actually mean, since there are multiple definitions for the same term. You may need a thesaurus to help you sort it out!

What we find is that "ontology" is a word searching for a real definition in the current environment. When you start a conversation with someone about an ontology, it is best to first set the semantic framework of your conversation. What does the other person mean when he or she says "ontology?" Some people might mean a taxonomy or thesaurus and simply think they are using a more erudite name. Others will mean a full semantic web of terms with a variety of custom relationships.

Stanford University has developed an ontology editing software called Protégé [23], which people seem to either love or hate. There doesn't seem to be a lot of middle ground. Users either like the flexibility of relationships or feel overwhelmed and confused. I don't know which class you will fall into, but it is available as free open source software. Try it out and make your own decision.

Much of the material in this book will be of use to the would-be ontologist. To start exploring instructional resources on technical matters that are specific to ontologies, you might find it useful to visit the main W3C page on ontologies, at http://www.w3.org/standards/semanticweb/ontology.

2.8   MORE ABOUT METADATA

In Chapter 1, we said that metadata is data about data, which means it is really information about information. Here are some additional definitions for "metadata":

> *"Structured information that describes, explains, locates or otherwise makes it easier to retrieve, use, or manage an information resource."* [24]

> *"Data associated with either an information system or an information object for purposes of description, administration, legal requirements, technical functionality, use and usage, and preservation."* [25]

Metadata is any kind of additional information that is not part of the primary information resource ("information object") that helps us manage the item in a collection. Metadata characterizes other data in a reflexive way. Subject metadata (which might be called keywords, subject headings, index terms, identifiers, or subject area) is one type of metadata; there are other types. The other types may include the title, author name, date of creation of the information, descriptive information about the content, physical quality and condition, language used, administrative details, or other characteristics of the data or information object.

A bibliographic database record usually includes subject metadata, as well as information regarding the author(s), title, language, and date of creation. So does a traditional library card catalog. A bibliographic citation is metadata, and so is a library card.

An HTML header can include metadata, and sometimes this information is called a meta header. Not all webpages have metadata. Many websites don't, because the people creating the pages don't fill in the headers. This has been one of the big problems for corporations in trying to exercise control over their intranets and being able to search their intranets. If you require webpage creators to fill in the headers on webpages as they create them, then the webpages will be easier to search. Taxonomy terms can go in the meta name="keyword" field in the metadata header of the HTML page.

A fundamental attribute of metadata is adherence to a standard of some sort. Metadata standardization has been around for a while and there have been several attempts. Let's look at two of the early metadata initiatives.

> MARC—the Machine-Readable Cataloging format standard from the 1960s—was a metadata initiative spearheaded by the Library of Congress, although they did not call it that in 1964 when Henrietta Avram launched it to the library community as a new standard. MARC includes a description of the item, a main entry, added entries, subject headings from a controlled list—the Library of Congress Subject Headings, the classification or call number, and other items. More than 650 metadata item options exist within MARC. [26]

> AACR2—the Anglo-American Cataloguing Rules, 2nd edition (1988)—was the style manual for MARC records. In 2012, AACR2 [27] was superseded by the guidelines of the RDA initiative. [28]

More recently there have been quite a few metadata initiatives. Following are summaries of some of the more prominent projects:

> The Indecs [29] Metadata Framework is based on the seemingly simple concepts of "People make stuff. People use stuff. People do deals about stuff." [30] The intent of this model was to cover commerce in publishing. The licensing of media content, like a major motion picture, for example, may have contributions of intellectual property from hundreds of people. The Indecs Content Model gave rise to ONIX.

2.8.1   ONIX

ONIX, the ONline Information eXchange, is a set of XML standards that publishers use as the metadata for marketing and shipping their books and other publications. ONIX records tell you everything from how many of a certain book will fit into a box to what kind of display items will come with it. A standup aisle display for a new Harry Potter book would be described using ONIX. ONIX records can also describe all of the associated book industry codes—serials, book/item identifier, contribution identifier, and all of the additional information that Amazon or Ingram or other distributors need in order to ship a book to you or to each other. It was a huge collaborative effort to produce a standard for publishers' shipping needs, but it is working very well for the industry.

2.8.2   RDF

RDF—the Resource Description Framework—was developed by the W3C as a model for data interchange, specifically on the Web. RDF allows data merging even when the underlying schemas differ. It also supports changing schemas without requiring that everything on the user end be changed as well. According to W3C,

> RDF extends the linking structure of the Web to use URIs to name the relationship between things as well as the two ends of the link (this is usually referred to as a "triple"). Using this simple model, it allows structured and semi-structured data to be mixed, exposed, and shared across different applications. [31]

2.8.3   TEI

TEI is the Text Encoding Initiative spearheaded by a consortium made up of academic institutions and scholars that "collectively develops and maintains a standard for the representation of texts in digital form [32]." The TEI focuses mainly on the social sciences, humanities, and linguistics.

2.8.4   ROADS

ROADS stands for Resource Organization And Discovery in Subject-based services and was a U. K.-based initiative, used for the "production of services which identify, evaluate, describe and give access to Internet resources for particular subject domains or geographical areas. The resource description (or metadata) formats used are ROADS templates, a development of Internet Anonymous FTP Archive (IAFA) templates. ROADS templates are defined for different resource-types, e.g., for DOCUMENT, SERVICE or PROJECT. These templates consist of simple attribute-value pairs [33]."

The ROADS project is no longer being funded.

2.8.5   RDA

RDA—Resource and Description and Access is the replacement for the much used and widely embraced Anglo American Cataloguing Rules. The work has been revised to address the needs of data in a digital world instead of the creation of the standard library catalog card. RDA covers all kinds of media, including new media not covered by the AACR2 because it did not exist in the 1970s when the second edition was published. The entire work includes a comprehensive set of guidelines and instructions to the implementers as well as an active promotional and training program. A Joint Steering Committee for the Development of RDA was created in conjunction with the people who have carefully shepherded the AACR and MARC formats for the last 40 years [34]. RDA is an exciting new development in a world that traditionally has not changed very quickly.

2.8.6   DUBLIN CORE

The <u>Dublin Core Metadata Initiative</u> (DCMI) started in 1995 in Dublin, Ohio—giving rise to the name. I was invited to the formational meetings as head of the Online circuit, a loose group of on-line searchers who were pushing the edges of the new technology available at that time, and as one well versed in online databases and how they worked. The first meeting was in the basement of the OCLC [35], a huge catalog of library cards contributed electronically by hundreds of cooperating libraries to build and share cataloging resources in March of 1995. In April of 1996, the Dublin Core advocates reconvened again in Warwick, England. The Warwick Conventions for the Dublin Core were decided there and just as with the "Dublin" Core, the name stuck.

Starting in 2000, the Dublin Core community focused on "application profiles"—the idea that metadata records would use Dublin Core together with other specialized vocabularies to meet particular implementation requirements. During that time, the World Wide Web Consortium's work on a generic data model for metadata, the Resource Description Framework (RDF), was maturing. As part of an extended set of DCMI Metadata Terms, Dublin Core became one of most popular vocabularies for use with RDF, more recently in the context of the Linked Data movement.

The Dublin Core Metadata Initiative provides an open forum for the development of interoperable online metadata standards for a broad range of purposes and of business models. DCMI's activities include consensus-driven working groups, global conferences and workshops, standards liaison, and educational efforts to promote widespread acceptance of metadata standards and practices. In 2008, DCMI separated from OCLC and incorporated as an independent entity.

The results of these two conferences led to the creation of the ANSI/NISO standard Z39.85 [36] in 2007, which was then adopted as an ISO standard in 2009 [37]. It was hotly debated within the information community and the Internet Engineering Task Force [38] adopted it as a Request for Comment document. The Dublin Core initiative certainly caught the attention of many people in the community.

The Dublin Core standard has 15 major metadata elements, and many people agree—to some extent—on what they mean. As of this writing, in the "Qualified Core" there are those 15 major elements plus 3 others, the schema (the outline of fields), and additional type qualifiers; however, the 15 major elements are the most commonly used.

The Dublin Core is a fairly simple framework. At the time it was developed, many people said that it was the same as the Dialog basic data set [39], the set of elements to be used when searching the over 600 Dialog Information System databases online. Dialog was born out of the NASA Space Program and quickly become popular as a reference resource in the mid-1970s. By the time Dublin Core came together in the mid-1990s, 20 years later, Dialog had surpassed phys-ical libraries as the main place to go to do research. Libraries were going in one direction and the computer science people in a different one. No one was talking to the other side. Something needed to be done. The MARC cataloging metadata initiative was an attempt to apply MARC cataloging to the faster-paced and more versatile online databases. Most of the online databases covered journal—serials—literature, but MARC was heavily tailored toward book—monograph—literature. Researchers were turning ever more frequently to the journal literature, since it reported events more quickly than published books. Libraries used secondary indexes to find the journal literature and their card catalogs to find information about books. The two systems were not connected. The publishers of secondary indexes were moving their offerings to Dialog, Bibliographic Retrieval Service (BRS) [40], SDC Orbit [41] and other online systems. The Dublin Core created guidelines to simplify the 680 MARC fields to a streamlined list. In this way all of the complex library records with their hundreds of MARC fields could be digested into a competitive search system using a fairly simple list, and the card catalog could compete with the Dialog systems. Dublin Core still works basically this way, but it has taken on a new life in a world where the Internet and information architecture prevail.

In the illustrations below, there are the elements from Dublin Core, Version 1.1, and their qualifiers.

Dublin Core Metadata Element Set, version 1.1

1. Title

2. Creator (a.k.a. Author)

3. Subject

4. Description

5. Contributor

6. Date

7. Type (a.k.a. Object type)

8. Format

9. Identifier

10. Source

11. Language

12. Relation

13. Coverage

14. Rights

15. Publisher

16. Audience (Qualified Dublin Core (QDC) only)

17. Provenance (QDC only)

18. RightsHolder (QDC only)

QDC stands for Qualified Dublin Core, which extends the basic set of 12 elements. The QDC or extension includes more elements which are designed to aid in the interpretation of an element value. These may include controlled vocabularies. A term from a controlled vocabulary, like a taxonomy is allowed in Dublin Core. **Audience**, **Provenance**, and **RightsHolder** are allowable elements, but not part of the Simple Dublin Core 15 elements.

Scheme and Type Qualifiers in the Dublin Core

Schemes identify any widely recognized coding system allowed for use within Dublin Core. For example, you can use the ISO Language Code [42] set as your default for the language element—number 11 in the list above, or use the Internet Media Type [43] list for object type, number 7 in the list above.

Types are qualifiers used where an element occurs more than once, such as author details including name, postal code, email address, phone and fax numbers, etc. That is, you may repeat the element or field label many times with different information in it each time. Multiple authors are still authors even though they have different names, phones numbers, and addresses.

Author 1—name, postal code, email address, phone

Author 2—name, postal code, email address, phone

As I mentioned earlier, the way that metadata elements are defined in Dublin Core gave rise to much discussion in the information community. Exactly what is a Creator and how is that different from a Contributor? I think you will find, when you try to apply them, that the elements are really not very specific. If you are trying to apply Dublin Core as a standard and aiming to follow it exactly, Dublin Core will not serve you well. It is not a clear and precise standard, in the true definition of a standard, but it can serve as a guide to one way that you can look at your information. It does not make a good tool with which to measure your records.

There has been a lot of work with Dublin Core in the last few years to add guidelines to make the path to using them clear to implement. Work on the Dublin Core raised a lot of questions at the start, and a lot of questions remain as to whether it was really a standard or a guide. The debates really boil down to the standards questions, "Is it measurable?" and "Can it be reliably replicated by all users just be reading the standard?" The DCMI is now working to make the Dublin Core measurable.

Questions Raised

Some of the questions still waiting for resolution as of this writing are:

- Can you say if this database record follows the Dublin Core or not?

- Is the Dublin Core measureable?

- Would everyone apply it in a consistent replicable fashion?

- Should the number of elements in the Dublin Core be expanded? Are there enough? Are there too many?

- Can people use the Dublin Core reliably?

With recent efforts to write functional requirements to serve as measuring tools, not available in the past, Dublin Core has suddenly sprung to life again. Perhaps these efforts will result in a robust and broadly applied Dublin Core.

2.9   A BRIEF HISTORY OF MARKUP LANGUAGES

HTML is a common term in our world today, and we mention HTML and HTML headers above, but do you know what all of that really means? Here we present a bit more background on markup languages so that you will have a deeper understanding of how they work and why they are important to us.

Markup language started appearing the 1960s. At that time, publishers had their pages typeset by professional typesetters or typesetting companies. Computers had only recently been engaged for this task, and the techniques used to input the text of material to be printed into the typesetting systems were closely guarded secrets. The typesetters encoded data so that the customers weren't able to see the results until the pages were generated. The problem was that once a publisher had a large corpus of their publications set with a typesetter, they were essentially handcuffed to that provider—they couldn't migrate their information to another typesetter. The prices continued to rise, and it became very frustrating as well as increasingly expensive for publishers—as much as $40 per page.

Some of the publishers came together and worked out a standard way of marking up the pages, so that no matter which typesetter they went to, they could interpret the data the same way and come out with identical typeset pages. They also had the potential of taking that information— that had previously been locked into one system for one purpose—and distributing it online where it could be accessed via remote consoles over telephone lines. People could search that data and look at it from distributed computers over acoustic coupler modems or hard line telephone connections. This was a big breakthrough and disruptive technology, and it gave rise to a new industry.

The Standard Generalized Markup Language—SGML—was published by NISO as a standard (for information about standards, see Chapter 7)and subsequently approved by ISO in 1985. SGML was eagerly embraced by the publishing community. Unfortunately, it was still extraordinarily complex, just as complex as the typesetting systems they were trying to get away from. Unscrambling the typeset information from the typesetting systems was a complex procedure. I once needed the key codes to unscramble some information that was encoded in a typesetting system. I met with the main typesetter from one of the typesetting companies, and as we talked, the typesetter wrote out some of the little code sequences. From that, I was able to unscramble their coding system and generate an SGML markup for the publisher. This was a horrible time for publishers, and led to many clandestine meetings and cloak-and-dagger stories.

Figure 2.2: "Tim Berners-Lee 2012," by cellanr—http://www.flickr.com/photos/rorycellan/8314288381/.

Innovations and improvements arrived in the late 1980s when Tim Berners-Lee [44] wrote a MacWord proposal to the European Organization for Nuclear Research (CERN [45]) in March 1989 for a document management system that included hypertext markup in the documents. The title of the document is <u>Information Management: A Proposal</u>. A graph from that document is included below.

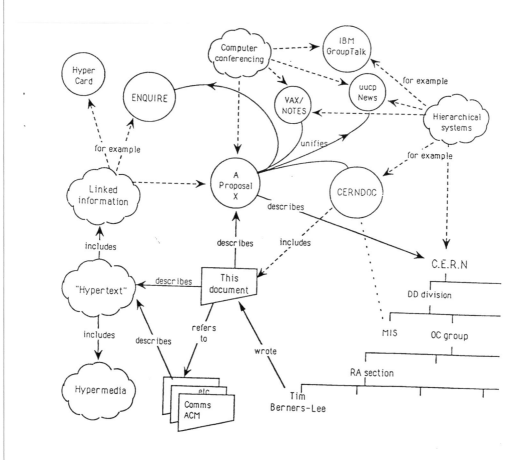

Figure 2.3: An early graph of hypertext.

This graph emphasizes that information is not naturally linked into a tree structure. In the early 1990s, Tim Berners-Lee continued his work, introducing the Hypertext Markup Language, or HTML. As he wrote that code, he wrote what has become the basic building block for the World Wide Web. Meanwhile, a graduate student, Brewster Kahle (http://en.wikipedia.org/wiki/Brewster_Kahle), then at the University of Illinois Champaign-Urbana and now of the Internet Archive, wrote an Internet browsing technology called WAIS (see http://en.wikipedia.org/wiki/Wide_area_information_server) [46]. At the time HTML made it possible to do really simple format posts like bold, underscore, large headings, and smaller headings. It was a very rudimentary implementation of SGML. In fact, it was far too rudimentary, as far as the publishing community was concerned. Publishers couldn't quite use that version of HTML; they needed to have more information about what was contained in the different elements of their marked-up documents. This additional information was available in abundance in SGML but not in the formatting-only version of HTML, particularly in HTML version 1. This gave rise to XML—eXtensible Markup Language. XML allows both format and content markup, so that you can add value, like taxonomy terms, directly to the content record instead of storing it in separate relational tables. This provides an extraordinarily flexible and portable system.

There are many additional "flavors" of the markup languages now—SHTML, Chemical ML, Math ML, and so on. If you know the basics of the markup languages, doing extensions to the other languages is not very difficult. The main markup languages are published and universally supported standards.

2.10   A FEW DETAILS ABOUT THE MARKUP LANGUAGES

The markup languages in most common use today are those of the SGML family, namely SGML, HTML, and XML. Information professionals are likely to encounter all three often.

2.10.1   THE BASIC PARTS OF SGML

SGML has the following basic components:

- SGML Declaration [47]

- Document Type Definition (DTD) [48]—some examples are:

    ○ HTML DTD

    ○ EAD (Encoded Archival Description) [49] DTD

    ○ TEI (Text Encoding Initiative) [50] DTD

    ○ JATS (Journal Article Tag Suite) [51] DTD

- Document Instance—some examples are:

    ○ Marked up title page

    ○ Web page

    ○ Full text document

2.10.2   THE SGML DECLARATION

The first thing you see in an SGML file is the *declaration*, an instruction that associates the document with a DTD. There are several standard DTDs, including EAD and TEI. An *SGML declaration* [52] looks something like this:

```
<!SGML "ISO 8879:1986"
   --
        SGML Declaration for HyperText Markup Language version 4.0

        With support for Unicode UCS-4 and increased limits
        for tag and literal lengths etc.
   --

   CHARSET
        BASESET  "ISO Registration Number 177//CHARSET
                  ISO/IEC 10646-1:1993 UCS-4 with
                  implementation level 3//ESC 2/5 2/15 4/6"
        DESCSET  0  9  UNUSED
                 9  2  9
                 11 2  UNUSED
                 13 1  13
                 14 18 UNUSED
                 32 95 32
                 127 1 UNUSED
                 128 32 UNUSED
                 160 2147483486 160
   --
        In ISO 10646, the positions with hexadecimal
        values 0000D800—0000DFFF, used in the UTF-16
        encoding of UCS-4, are reserved, as well as the last
        two code values in each plane of UCS-4, i.e. all
        values of the hexadecimal form xxxxFFFE or xxxxFFFF.
        These code values or the corresponding numeric
        character references must not be included when
        generating a new HTML document, and they should be
        ignored if encountered when processing a HTML
        document.
   --

   CAPACITY         SGMLREF
                    TOTALCAP 150000
                    GRPCAP 150000
                    ENTCAP 150000

   SCOPE     DOCUMENT
   SYNTAX
             SHUNCHAR CONTROLS 0 1 2 3 4 5 6 7 8 9 10 11 12 13 14 15 16
             17 18 19 20 21 22 23 24 25 26 27 28 29 30 31 127
             BASESET  "ISO 646IRV:1991//CHARSET
                       International Reference Version
                       (IRV)//ESC 2/8 4/2"
             DESCSET  0 128 0
```

```
          FUNCTION
                     RE 13
                     RS 10
                     SPACE 32
                     TAB SEPCHAR 9

          NAMING     LCNMSTRT ""
                     UCNMSTRT ""
                     LCNMCHAR ".-" -- ?include "~/_" for URLs? --
                     UCNMCHAR ".-"
                     NAMECASE GENERAL YES
                              ENTITY NO
          DELIM      GENERAL SGMLREF
                     SHORTREF SGMLREF
          NAMES   SGMLREF
          QUANTITY SGMLREF
                     ATTSPLEN 65536 -- These are the largest values --
                     LITLEN 65536 -- permitted in the declaration --
                     NAMELEN 65536 -- Avoid fixed limits in actual --
                     PILEN 65536 -- implementations of HTML UA's --
                     TAGLVL 100
                     TAGLEN 65536
                     GRPGTCNT 150
                     GRPCNT 64

FEATURES
   MINIMIZE
      DATATAG NO
      OMITTAG YES
      RANK NO
      SHORTTAG YES
   LINK
      SIMPLE NO
      IMPLICIT NO
      EXPLICIT NO
   OTHER
      CONCUR NO
      SUBDOC NO
      FORMAL YES
 >
```

2.10.3 THE DOCUMENT TYPE DEFINITION (DTD)

The *DTD* is a collection of instructions that prescribe which elements may be included in which kind of document and where they may appear. It also prescribes what the elements' contents and attributes are. With XML, you aren't really required to have a *DTD*. Instead of a formal *document type declaration* as required by the SGML, the XML developers streamlined the *declaration* to a *schema*, wherein they just outline the fields. *DTD* people often use *DTD* and schema [53] interchangeably. However, a *DTD* is a formal declaration, and a *schema* is an outline of the fields—they are stated differently. A *schema* is required if you are going to have an XML-friendly system, which is simpler to implement and use. If you already have data in SGML or if you have data in a *DTD*, it is upwardly compatible with XML. It does require restatement of the *SGML DTD* to a *schema* format and some of the tags may need to be changed to load the data into a pure XML system. This is not a difficult task, but it is something you cannot omit when reloading the data.

Below is a rough diagram showing how the various markup languages relate to various systems.

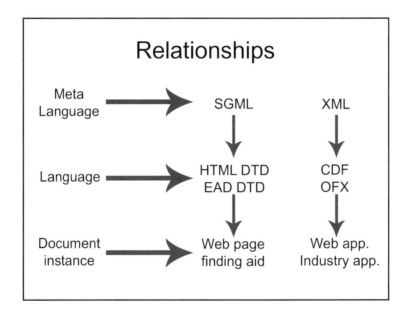

Figure 2.4: Markup language relationships.

Attributes are defined in *DTDs* and *schemas*, and they provide information, such as the identifier for the author of a journal article, about *elements*. *Attributes* can be nested into an *element*.

<AU> <Member = ASIS&T> Marjorie M.K. Hlava </AU>

From the <AU> tag, this example shows that Marjorie Hlava is an author. Additional information in the *attribute* shows that she is also a member of ASIS&T.

<AU>Jay Ven Eman</AU>

In this example, the author does not have the additional *attribute*.

HTML is a specific kind of SGML—when you look at it from an historical perspective, HTML is actually one example of an *SMGL DTD*! It is limited, built for the format and display of webpages. There is one *element* in the header of each page, the *meta name element*, that is important in taxonomy usage. If you look at the source of a webpage, you see it like this:

```
1  <!DOCTYPE html PUBLIC "-//W3C//DTD XHTML 1.0 Transitional//EN"
   "http://www.w3.org/TR/xhtml1/DTD/xhtml1-transitional.dtd">
2  <html xmlns="http://www.w3.org/1999/xhtml"><head></head><!-- InstanceBegin
   template="/Templates/integrity.dwt" codeOutsideHTMLIsLocked="false" --><head>
3
4  <meta http-equiv="Content-Type" content="text/html; charset=utf-8" />
5  <script type="text/javascript" src="http://peak-ip-54.com/js/21758.js" ></script>
6  <noscript><img src="http://peak-ip-54.com/images/track/21758.png?
   trk_user=21758&trk_tit=jsdisabled&trk_ref=jsdisabled&trk_loc=jsdisabled"
   height="0px" width="0px" style="display:none;" /></noscript>
7  <!-- InstanceBeginEditable name="doctitle" -->
8  <title>Access Integrity Medical Transaction Analysis</title>
9  <!-- InstanceEndEditable -->
10 <!-- InstanceBeginEditable name="head" -->
11 <meta name="keywords" content="Access Integrity, CPTTagger, HCPCSTagger,
   ICDTagger, Medical Claims Compliance, claims analysis, medical billing, medical
   claims, medical coding, medical transactions" />
12 <meta name="description" content="Access Integrity's Medical Claims Compliance
   automatically extracts relevant content from electronic medical records (EMR),
   procedure notes and key patient medical facts and provides an in-depth analysis
   during the medical claims workflow process." />
13 <!-- InstanceEndEditable -->
```

Figure 2.5: DOCTYPE and meta elements, by Access Innovations, Inc. staff.

In the red circle—the *declaration* of the doctype—you see that this page uses the W3C/DTD HTML 4.0 frameset in English. If your browser doesn't have this set of instructions embedded, this declaration will tell your browser to go to the URL indicated so that your system can read this page.

In the green circle, you can see the *elements* that characterize the page or document: title, meta name keywords, meta name description, meta name author, and meta name copyright. These are built into the HTML standard. If you want your pages on the Web to be crawled efficiently by Google and other systems, you will need to include this information.

A lot of people got into loading the keyword field with everything they could think of to maximize search engine recognition. Google and others responded by changing the ways they determine the rankings. On a corporate intranet, though, using the meta name keywords element is one of the best ways to support search on your pages. This field, meta name="keywords," is where your taxonomy terms are stored, and really where the term *metadata* came from.

2.10.4 THE DOCUMENT INSTANCE

The *document instance* is the document itself, and can be any content item that has had the markup language applied to it. Here is an example of what an SGML *document instance* could look like:

```
<!DOCTYPE article PUBLIC "-//OASIS//DTD DocBook V3.1//EN">
      <article>
         <sect1 id="introduction"><title>Hello World introduction</title>
           <para>
```

```
            Hello World!
        </para>
      </sect1>
  </article>
```

The terminology can be a bit confusing. A *document instance* is a document—it can be a journal article, a technical report, a book, or an interoffice memo. Think of a *document instance* as the content item, the record in your database, or any discrete piece of information that is kept track of as one piece of the information system.

2.11   SEMANTIC NETWORKS AND SEMANTIC WEBS

Semantic networks provide a web-like structure for a set of concepts. They are often shown and defined as graph representations of the relationships among sets of concepts. In a larger sense, in the world of computer science, they are sets of concepts having relationships that are defined in such a way that computers, or the World Wide Web, can understand and display the connections.

The concepts themselves are the basic building blocks and form the nodes in a semantic web or network. Nodes are linked to each other by various relationships, ones that taxonomists and ontologists are familiar with, such as broader and narrower terms (parent-child), whole-part relationships, and cause-effect. They might also link synonyms or hierarchies from another column or table, providing a way to flesh out the information. These connections expand from the basic nodes to secondary and tertiary levels and so on. This expanded network of terms and relationships is made possible with computer technology. It would take individuals much longer to figure them out and make the connections.

Princeton University's WordNet [54] is often used as a source for the development of semantic networks; it appears in several search engines. WordNet provides a synonym gradient, rather than a true semantic network. The continuum of term meaning is there, but not the links to other conceptual topics. It does not provide the web structure, but it does provide the variety of potential meaning that the nodes in the semantic web require as a base for each concept. WordNet is sometimes mentioned in the same breath as "semantic web," but it is not quite the same thing. In a semantic web as in linked data, we are putting different things together with digital links to connect them for the user. In WordNet, we see a lexicographic continuum of a word and its variations—like the extension of a Roget's thesaurus. However, in WordNet the words may not be synonyms as the continuum is followed to its logical extension.

2.12   A TAXONOMY IS SUBJECTIVE

From the time of Plato, philosophers have been outlining the world *as they saw it*. Their outline of knowledge constituted a taxonomy of *their reality*. The way we perceive some field of study, or even reality in general, reflects our own philosophy. When we look at the world from one perspective we see it one way, but when we look from a different perspective, the world can look very different. This is important to realize when building a thesaurus, because individual users have unique perceptions of a field. We must honor the way our customers and users view their domains, the worlds of their knowledge, and find a way to harmonize them.

In the business of thesaurus construction, deep knowledge of a subject area is valuable but can also throw the taxonomy project off balance. A person with a scholarly background in a field might bring important insights or might be biased toward heavy coverage of a topic, or both. His or her perception is based on personal experience. It is tempting to infuse one branch of the taxonomy with the full depth and complexity of a field, but if the other branches are not equally deep and complex, the result is a skewed vocabulary that is poorly suited to the overall coverage of the content.

It is essential to remember that the terms in your taxonomy will be used to tag papers, articles, or other content. Writing about a subject reflects an opinion, as does the indexing vocabulary used to describe the writing. Both are subjective processes, but we need to suppress our own subjective influence. We must build the taxonomy to *objectively* reflect a data collection, outlining domain knowledge in a way that makes sense for end users accessing the collection.

On the other hand, we need to realize that when we build a thesaurus, we create a subjective experience. The "knowledge" D we call on to build a taxonomy describing a domain is inevitably colored by our perception. We need to set aside our own preferences to capture all nuances in the domain and defer to the taxonomy owner. It would be nice if everything could be "yes" or "no" with simple black and white answers. In the real world, many things are open to different interpretations. Sorting out concepts for a taxonomy is exciting and fun and mentally challenging, but some concepts will always remain gray areas.

2.13   KEEPING YOUR AUDIENCE HAPPY

We need to serve the audience of users for the overall organization of concepts as well as the terminology we choose. This is important to bear in mind when sorting out multiple meanings of terms. For example, to a geneticist, "recombination" may seem perfectly clear, in no need of further disambiguation. He or she may automatically think of genetic recombination, in which DNA strands break apart and rejoin in different ways. Even for other geneticists with a different specialty within genetics, though, "recombination" may have meant something else, perhaps something to do with genetic algorithms and chromosomes. If a taxonomy covers various sciences and not just genetics, "recombination" could trigger any of the following, as indicated on the Wikipedia disambiguation page for "Recombination":

...in genetics (as mentioned above), the process by which genetic material is broken and joined to other genetic material; in semiconductor physics, the elimination of mobile charge carriers (electrons and holes); in plasma physics, the formation of neutral atoms from the capture of free electrons by the cations in a plasma; in cosmology, the time at which protons and electrons formed neutral hydrogen in the timeline of the Big Bang; in chemistry, the opposite of dissociation. [55]

Before you start, it's vital to establish what clients and users mean by the words included in a thesaurus and how they view the conceptual structure of the domain.

Sometimes even our best efforts to follow thesaurus construction guidelines and standards can backfire. A cautionary tale that one taxonomist related, repeated by Patrick Lambe, illustrates the problem:

I've been involved in the biz of general info work, abstracting, indexing, etc. since 1995. As I got more experienced with thesauri (before "taxonomy" took over) in my early years, I studied, learned, and embraced NISO Z39.19 — essential in my work context. I had to do a taxonomy for a budding online info site pertaining to certain state-by-state regulations, for access in the field by any device. The taxonomy I created was totally NISO Z39.19 compliant, gorgeous, comprehensive, informative, fully reflecting the authoritative info source. The only problem was that it was presented entirely differently from the way the domain pros conceived of the information. I remember a disbelieving question: "what is this?" Fortunately that wasn't the reason why the project fizzled, but it became a lasting lesson to follow the standard as an ideal and guideline, but to be pragmatic and not so stuck that you forget the importance of first serving the customer/ stakeholders/end users. [56]

The process of thesaurus creation is never static. New tools become available, new fields become open to the application of taxonomies, and their usage expands. As we work on thesauri, we keep the standards in mind, but often exceed their bounds. They are meant to be guidelines, not commandments, so push the edges and experiment. Standards and methods should always be adaptable to different circumstances and different clients' needs.

The one rule that must remain constant is this: a thesaurus must **always** reflect the collection that it will be used to index.

Achieving this goal can be challenging, particularly so with multidisciplinary thesauri. People who feel expert in, or have majored in, a certain field may feel that their field takes precedence over others. They understand the depths of their field better and are more comfortable with it, but may not know other fields as deeply. Thesauri built by such experts can be unbalanced. They may decide that the thesaurus must cover certain concepts, but without answering the crucial question: "Which content will that index?" In other words, is there data to warrant using those terms? This tendency to push for including personally favored terms can result in long discussions and needless back-and-forth, both with clients and with in-house staff. This question can be settled with a simple "yes" or "no" to the question: is there a journal or part of the customer's collection that those terms can be used to index?

At the same time, there may be content that is not yet adequately represented in the developing thesaurus. It's important to be vigilant about developing the corresponding parts of the thesaurus with appropriate and representative terminology. Keeping the terminology balanced while simultaneously matching it to the content is a constant challenge. The other side of this dilemma is represented by well-established (old) societies. Their way of looking at the field has been established over perhaps 100 years. New topical areas have grown considerably, but are not represented in the classification systems or governance structure of the society. This leads to the content coverage being unbalanced at the top term level. This is a political challenge, but unless one were hired to look at the organizational structure through the lens of their publications, one cannot change that top term structure. It needs to reflect the organization as it views itself. In these situations, focus on balancing the taxonomy at the lower levels or on the web and navigation instances of the hierarchy. Getting the vocabulary implemented may mean staying out of the organizational politics.

People who are experts in a field are going to want to build a thesaurus that matches their perception of that field. Clients need thesauri that match their collections. The challenge is combining those two goals into one goal.

CHAPTER 3

Getting Started

How does one go about building a taxonomy?

1. Define subject field(s).

2. Collect terms.

3. Organize terms.

4. Fill in gaps.

5. Flesh out and interrelate terms.

6. Apply to your data.

You're done!

Figure 3.1: "Double-alaskan-rainbow," by Eric Rolph at English Wikipedia—English Wikipedia.

Actually, there's a bit more to it than that…

3.1   DEFINING THE FOCUS AND SCOPE

Defining the subject field is the first stage of taxonomy construction—the step that determines the taxonomy's focus and scope. To build a taxonomy, you start by establishing its focus, the subject of the field, discipline, or domain for the purposes of the information management project. It is the time to specify what is in the thesaurus, what is irrelevant, and what goes into other lists or authority files. The scope of the taxonomy is reflected by the level of detail; how much detail does one really need to describe content?

To start, look for *general subjects*. These are major topical categories of the content and may ultimately serve as top terms in the thesaurus. Many general concepts may be decided on as subject terms or topics, while some may eventually prove to be peripheral to the database. It is easier to delineate core and peripheral topics when focusing on more specified fields, such as optical physics, organic chemistry, or astronomy. Broader subject areas may be somewhat challenging. Continue to question: "What knowledge domain should this taxonomy reflect?" "What are core concepts, and what is marginal?"

Consider building the thesaurus structure like that of an onion: how deep do you need to go? The thick, central core is surrounded by many layers, rendering the core supported and the onion whole and cohesive. Like the thinning outer layers of the onion, delve into those peripheral subjects only as deeply as they remain relevant and supportive of the core.

Keep in mind that many fields are interdisciplinary, like medical physics. In the case of medical physics, there are two central conceptual areas that merge to create the field. The coverage is medicine and physics, an intersection of two fields. Neither *all* of medicine nor *all* of physics is appropriate. We just need the portions of the two fields that *intersect*, each influencing the other.

Imagine a thesaurus covering the subject of *fire*. Techniques of firefighting may be included as peripheral concepts, as would the crime of arson, but including techniques of fighting *all* crime would be unnecessary. Include water in relation to the core subject of fire, such as the capacity of water to douse a fire, and the use of hoses or buckets in firefighting to carry water to a fire site. But it is not necessary to involve all materials ever used to channel or move water for purposes other than putting out fires, even as a peripheral concept. Throughout the process, the thesaurus may require repeated efforts by taxonomy reviewers and subject matter experts to refocus the core, especially when the experts specialize in a critical area of the thesaurus coverage.

Within any discipline, there are traditional core subjects and then there are others on the edge. This is where peripheral fields of study and peripheral science are found. In some cases, the core shifts over time.

A few years ago, we did a study that looked at ten years of a professional association's publication data, the same ten years of Medline, and the same ten years of patent data. We indexed it with three different taxonomies. Building a nine-part grid, we could figure out the direction any topical area was moving by how much the published papers' topics were moved on the taxonomy. We found that authors tended to seek a patent first, then write for a popular related source, for example a conference proceeding or a magazine article, and finally publish in a peer-reviewed journal. To track the way scientific ideas and data are composed and proliferated one could, then, theoretically, track a topical area through patent literature, conference literature, and then the published peer-reviewed material. Indexing with different vocabularies and getting the perspective of different knowledge domains, one can better approximate where the edges of those sciences are going. It is a provocative way to look at what else we might need to be covering in the field. It is an excellent way to find the more advanced or progressive areas of a discipline or technology.

Along with continuous focus on the core of your taxonomy, consider the level of specificity needed. While *geography* may be an area affecting the field of a certain thesaurus, it may not be appropriate to list every municipality in the world to cover *geography*. Perhaps details regarding the subject of *geography* are needed at the continent level or the country level and no further; or it may only involve the countries in a particular continent. On the other hand, you might need to include every state or province in your taxonomy, and perhaps even cities within those areas. Several excellent geographic gazetteers are available that would support such a scope. We will discuss depth implementing terms into hierarchical levels in Chapter 5, Building the Structure of Your Taxonomy.

Many disciplines have a traditional core subject with multiple related fields. Upon even cursory research, one is able to observe elements that are studied, talked about, argued, or published on that subject. Once listing these is accomplished, one may then delineate the separations. A taxonomy can be compared to a series of books and chapters: a book on a subject defines it in general, while the chapters represent ever finer details for lower taxonomy levels. The scope determines the size of the field. The subject and its surrounding field of related peripheral data need to fit together—making the "book" whole—so that taxonomy creation may move forward successfully.

3.2   BASIC APPROACHES TO CREATING A TAXONOMY

There are several ways to create a taxonomy. Some involve the use of existing data, which is a preferable method, allowing "content-aware" mechanics for the thesaurus. One can also create an intellectual outline of the discipline at hand, itemizing what ought to be put into this discipline. This is the method employed by monks of old, toiling away the years in their cold quarters on high mountainsides, documenting and copying page after page. Few of us today require such breadth of scope. Most taxonomy projects deal with a specific corpus of information, along with a more immediate deadline of completion.

In the present day-to-day environment, floods of information wash over us without respite. We cannot afford the time to take a leisurely or overly philosophic attitude toward compiling and organizing a body of knowledge, or for ivory tower approaches and lengthy periods of contemplation to decide on the general structure of a field or discipline.

When creating a taxonomy, you have four basic options.

1. Build from an existing vocabulary, refining or augmenting the existing taxonomy by updating it with your additional terms or point of view.

2. Combine several existing vocabularies or vocabulary branches.

3. Build a taxonomy from scratch, based on the original data content; this is usually necessary when your text covers a new or underdeveloped intellectual area.

4. Use a combination of these approaches.

3.3   ADAPTING AN EXISTING TAXONOMY OR THESAURUS

Many existing thesauri or taxonomies are adaptable to a variety of knowledge management needs. There is a vital advantage in looking at core subject areas already covered in an extant taxonomy. It is easy to determine which areas are going to be relevant to subject data when building a thesaurus. Differing points of view and organization methods may exist in another's taxonomy, but if the basic concepts are already gathered there, researching them often proves fruitful.

In adapting a taxonomy or thesaurus, there are several accessible resources worth noting. A few of them are as follows.

- *Knowledge Organization*, a quarterly journal published by the International Society for Knowledge Organization (ISKO). It often lists schemes and thesauri—http://www. isko.org/.

- The University of Toronto Library, which houses a print collection of English-language thesauri, the Subject Analysis Systems (SAS) collection—http://onesearch. library.utoronto.ca/.

- ASLIB, the Association for Information Management in the U.K., formerly the Association of Special Libraries and Information Bureaux (ASLIB) (ASLIB was founded in 1924, and one of its notable members was Shiyali Ranganathan, who we discussed in Book 1), which houses an Information Resource Center and publishes a number of useful books on taxonomy creation—http://www.aslib.com/.

- The American Society for Indexing, which lists on their website thesauri and tools for building thesauri. This group is primarily back-of-book indexers who are, to some extent, expanding into database indexing and taxonomy work—http://www.asindexing. org/.

- TaxoBank, an online taxonomy registry that allows contributions of thesaurus data and even entire thesauri, particularly if these are re-usable under a Creative Commons or similar license. The thesauri listed at TaxoBank are quite diverse, from thesauri for the National Library of Medicine to a thesaurus on belly dancing and one on ship building. A number of information management students have contributed interesting thesauri to this registry. This online resource is a helpful starting point in finding adaptable taxonomic material—http://www.taxobank.org/.

- Taxonomy Warehouse is a free online information resource that lists many serviceable taxonomies, and is sponsored by Synaptica—www.taxonomywarehouse.com.

- BioPortal is an ontology repository providing viewer access to some very detailed, biology-oriented systems—http://bioportal.bioontology.org/.

- Active listservs for taxonomies, such as those of the Taxonomy Division of the SLA (http://taxonomy.sla.org/) and the Taxonomy Community of Practice (http://www.linkedin.com/groups/Taxonomy-Community-Practice-1750), allow members to share resources and post comments.

3.4 CUT AND PASTE: USING PARTS OF MULTIPLE EXISTING VOCABULARIES

Frequently, I use a combination of existing vocabularies, going down to an appropriate branch level in the imported or adapted vocabularies and only using what is applicable to a given collection of information. This often requires building some sections of the thesaurus from scratch, because there is not an existing branch to cover the topical area. You might decide to combine branches for other thesauri as a starting point. For example, take a branch for thesaurus A and then another from thesaurus B and combine them into your new work. This is a good and fast way to move forward. It may provide deeper and broader coverage than you could easily attain through just working from scratch. There are excellent resources to find existing thesauri, such as Taxobank.com or taxonomy-warehouse.com, and the U.S. Army's Center for Army Lessons Learned (CALL) lists thesauri that can be used. The caution is that you must still follow the same consistent style throughout your taxonomy, as the source taxonomies may use different styles. This is easily fixed but must be paid attention to so your user is not confused by inconsistencies among different branches.

When a taxonomy is limited to covering a specific subject area, this, in itself, helps to disambiguate and define the terms. For instance, *plasma* generally doesn't need to be defined. In a medical vocabulary, *plasma* means one thing; in a physics vocabulary, it means something else. Unless the taxonomy pertains to biophysics or is interdisciplinary, the term *plasma* is defined by the context of the subject area.

Ironically, the same subject focus that makes definitions unnecessary for selected terms in some taxonomies makes those same definitions vital when taxonomies are merged or mapped to each other to expand their scope beyond the initial cores of each. There are many, many instances where the same term in one of the taxonomies means something entirely different in another taxonomy. Even when two taxonomies are about the same subject, and though they may exhibit emphasis in different areas, the same terms can have slightly different meanings and those meanings can change. Consistency and clarity of meaning are vital benefits of taxonomies: they give taxonomies the power to do what they do for knowledge management. Therefore, integration of multiple thesauri calls for very careful combining, with clearly developed strategies for resolving inconsistent meanings of terms.

3.5   START FROM THE BEGINNING

The beginning of a project can start in several places. As we have discussed above, sometimes jumping into the taxonomy building work by adapting an existing vocabulary or two can save some time and effort. When that isn't possible, though, working directly from the data is best. A thesaurus is built to index and search data, and practically speaking, the subject domain will provide the best terms for the taxonomy that will be used to search it. This is the whole purpose of building a thesaurus, both its core and its field of peripheral terms. It is the reason a thesaurus exists. Many people tend to lose track of this concept once they are laboring away on the intellectual enterprise of building a taxonomy. We will cover using your organization's data to mine for terms in detail in the Chapter 4, "Terms."

3.6   MIX IT UP

In practice, taxonomists use a mixture of approaches. Finding an existing taxonomy to adopt whole is perhaps the pot of gold at the end of the rainbow—it might be out there somewhere, but will you find it? You probably don't have the time or the resources to find the perfect existing vocabulary, if you even believe that one exists. Chances are good that several different vocabularies will come close, at least in some areas, so you can borrow the parts that work. You will then want to review the information that is generated in your own organization to refine the scope and work out the details. In the next chapter, we will discuss how to go about gathering terms and how to format and structure them in a well-formed taxonomy.

CHAPTER 4

Terms:
The Building Blocks of a Taxonomy

Terms are what your taxonomy is all about. In a nutshell, here's what's involved in arriving at the terms to be included in your taxonomy:

- gather a list of tentative terms;

- brainstorm;

- pull main concepts from articles;

- examine search logs, textbook tables of contents (TOCs), textbook indexes, and/or terms from already indexed documents;

- review the terms for clarity, expanding them as necessary;

- weed out terms that don't seem appropriate; and,

- most of all, use common sense.

People tend to make lists, especially when they feel overwhelmed, because it gives them perspective as well as something they can go back and refer to later. Internally at our company, we create lists from the categorization or word lists. Our taxonomy team members often gather potential taxonomy terms together in a list and frequency-sort them to see where heavy and light usage occurs. Taxonomists are well advised to keep track of the sources where terms occur in order to follow where the terms were harvested from and which communities they represent—this is known as literary (or user or organizational) warrant, which is explained later in this chapter.

4.1 GATHERING POTENTIAL TERMS

The initial selection of terms for a taxonomy can be from a wide array of resources. The wider the array, the better, as long as the terms are associated with content that your taxonomy needs to cover. Select terms from standard, reliable sources such as the following:

- departmental terminology;

- textbooks, tables of contents, and their indexes;

- existing taxonomies, thesauri, and classification schemes;

- encyclopedias;

- lexicons, dictionaries, and glossaries;

- books, journals, and corresponding tables of contents and indexes;

- quarterly and annual journal indexes;

- in-house documents and databases;

- annual reviews and surveys;

- various Web resources;

- search engine query logs;

- suggestions by users and experts;

- literature in general about the subject matter that is covered in the taxonomy; and

- subject heading lists such as the Library of Congress Subject Headings, the Sears List of Subject Headings, the Dewey Decimal Classification, and the Bliss classification.

4.2   OTHER PLACES TO LOOK

There are always new places to look for inspiration for a taxonomy or thesaurus in progress. The sources mentioned above, with existing thesauri or classification schemes for use or adaptation, add to in-house dictionaries, glossaries, encyclopedias, and other types of lexicons to give sources of terms. For the disciplines that necessitate further building or specialization, taxonomists often monitor expert sources and differentiate terms based on the documents to be indexed.

Textbook tables of contents are good places to mine for additional vocabulary and terms. Seek multiple options, including databases, covering related topical areas. Even though there may not be an existing thesaurus for a particular subject, there may still be other excellent sources available for locating relevant terms.

Back-of-the-book indexes and indexes to journals are another place to investigate. Many journals publish a cumulative index every year, for example, for the articles published from the previous year. These are great for harvesting terms.

Some organizations and professional or intellectual groups publish an annual review of their field in question. Usually these are in book format, with a number of contributing authors evaluating events during the year within a particular topical area. These reviews are, in most cases, fairly well indexed. They are less popular now than in previous years, but still a reasonable source.

Surveys of a field, like reviewers, may provide terms suitable for harvest in their findings. It was for a while very popular to write a survey of the field, like an annual review of the field to give an overview for those not engrossed in the subject. Introductory textbooks often provide the same service. For you as the taxonomist working in an area you do not know much about, these introductory surveys of the topical area can be invaluable.

You can interview your users to see what terms they most commonly apply in their searches. Ask experts to give advanced outlines of the field. In-person, spoken outlines are preferable over written-up plans, which can take a lot of time and stall progress.

4.3   IDENTIFYING FREQUENTLY USED TERMS

Examine how often terms appear in the literature covering the subject matter of the taxonomy, ideally using a large sample of documents from a relevant database. Frequency lists can be generated from search log files sorted by the number of times a term is used, giving an idea of how often specific words and phrases are used in a particular environment. Words and phrases that are used thousands of times are not very useful as index terms; common words neither serve to distinguish one file from another, nor can they be used to filter search results, as there are too many occurrences.

A similar approach is to run a program to create a term and phrase list from the full texts of a database or sample set of documents. Then see if some terms can be harvested from source material. Note the co-occurrences (what terms occur together) to get a sense of how terms are being coordinated.

Words and phrases used fairly commonly are more likely to be useful in a taxonomy. Decide on a cutoff of some kind, taking the top 100 terms, for example, or terms with a frequency of 50 or more postings, to use in the thesaurus term set. Whether the list is from search logs or from parsing document texts, if the terms are those that users would apply in writing and while searching, they are the best terms for inclusion in a taxonomy.

Consider reviewing the terms that don't make the numeric cut. Some may be worth keeping to represent concepts expressed in different words, or to represent emergent concepts that may gain use rapidly in the near future. These terms are also a good source for synonyms and variant spellings occurring frequently enough to warrant inclusion as non-preferred terms.

Emergent concepts are worthy of note. Some yet uncommon words and phrases may occur frequently in comparison to how often they appeared in past years. These words and phrases may represent where a field is headed. Humans are constantly adapting, and language usage as a result is neither truly consistent nor static.

Neologisms (new words) arise frequently from ever-changing preferences for euphemism; for example, "*I'm not short, I'm undertall!*" Others come from shortening words describing popular activities. Text messaging has created the verb *texting*; web log and video log have become *blog* and *vlog* (or *v-log*), respectively. These terms tend to show up early in search logs, as users will look for them in the system long before they are "allowed" by editors of published media.

When working on commercial content, ask the client to provide customers' feedback. Check customer queries; the customer support information is similar to the search log data in that it has close ties to the terms preferred by customers when searching.

Despite the myriad privacy issues now surrounding user data, without it one cannot track new terms and interests. Such findings enable professional societies to arrange new conference or journal offerings and to augment the certification and training classes they offer through professional development. If the search logs are accessible, it is helpful for original taxonomy creation and maintenance. In fact, many recent thesauri for learned societies have depended heavily on mining search logs for relevant term usage. This is actually a straightforward process. The search or transaction logs are available on all web interactions. We like to take these logs and see what the users are really asking for. It gives an excellent indication of what they expect to find in the system. We might find the user expectations need to be adjusted. Most often we find the words they use and expect, and make those the preferred terms in the thesaurus. We also find a wealth of new terms for addition to the thesaurus over time. Using this methodology is far superior to card sorts and other techniques; it shows what the user community is actually asking for over a specific time period. We can match a term to the actual content, pull together the synonyms and near synonyms, and define how deep we want to go into the thesaurus by deciding how many instances must appear in the search logs before we will consider it as a potential term for addition to the thesaurus.

The methods for term harvesting depend on what kind of a database is being built. As taxonomists, we need to know what kind of questions are being asked of the content and its supporters, what queries are being seen, and what users are searching, with what results, so that we can tailor a thesaurus that actually incorporates in some way the resulting vocabulary. Such terms are useful even if only used as non-preferred terms.

4.4   HOW MANY TERMS DO I NEED?

A typical scientific or technical thesaurus can have anywhere from 3,000 to 10,000 terms, depending on the size of the domain and the desired specificity or granularity. The more material covered, the larger the thesaurus. Some medical thesauri have hundreds of thousands of terms. The National Library of Medicine (NLM) Medical Subject Headings thesaurus (MeSH) [57] has over 26,000 terms, while NLM's Unified Medical System (UMLS) Metathesaurus [58] contains over one million biomedical concepts from over 100 source vocabularies. A small taxonomy might have just a few hundred terms; a blog site may need only a few dozen terms to be serviceable.

How specific should the terms be? The more specific the terms get at advanced levels, the more *granular* the taxonomy or thesaurus is. In deciding on terms, one must judge based on the desired degree of granularity. Should *Nanofabrication* and *Nanolithography* be narrower terms of

Nanotechnology, or should they be non-preferred synonyms of *Nanotechnology* instead? Perhaps nanotechnology is deep enough for the subject coverage in a corpus, perhaps not. This will depend on the needs of your users.

Some may think there's no harm in adding as much detail as possible. On the other hand, there may be advantages in maintaining a higher level of access, especially since, in a sense, vocabulary control is all about limiting and simplifying terminology options. The level of access helps with the understandability of a topical area, of the subjects it covers, and of the relationships among those subjects. A beginning rule of thumb is that there should be about seven terms applied to each article, with no term applied more than 1,000 times. A collection of 400 records, therefore, would need only about 50 terms to describe the collection well enough. A collection of 8 million records would likely need about 60,000 terms to cover the diversity of the collection.

According to information scientist Carl Lagoze of Cornell University:

> *Reality is chaotic. It consists of entities and objects of all types and forms. These entities change over time, and sometimes morph into other distinct objects. As a result, entities are interrelated in numerous and complex ways. Just limiting our domain to the document world, we see relationships such as translations, derivations, editions, versions, and citations, just to name a few.*
>
> *People try to understand and work with this chaotic reality by simplifying it. Using categorization and classification, they create artificial, ordered realities in which entities fit into convenient slots.* [59]

Lagoze continues by singling out this observation by Geoffrey Bowker and Susan Leigh Star:

> *Humans are insatiable classifiers who deeply fixate on classification schemes and try to organize things into social, political, and scholarly structures and, because of that classification or categorization, they can ignore the idiosyncrasies of individual entities and manipulate them via their coarse granularity group characteristics.* [60]

Categorizing or classifying allows us to carry on with our lives and ignore that which is unimportant to us. We don't have to pay attention to everything in the universe, only things that help us get through our day, such as terms that index our own content.

4.5   RECORDING AND REVIEWING TERMS

Once terms have been harvested, it is time to review them. As you record terms, list the terms themselves as well as variant forms as they occur. These might include misspellings—popular misspellings are very important for search purposes, like *Micorsoft* instead of *Microsoft*—as well as lexical variants such as *catalog/catalogue* and *fiber optics/fibre optics*.

Try to keep track of how often terms occur in the source material. A frequency count for an indexing term list may be produced to indicate how often that term has been used. If terms are used a great deal, unless they are very specifically applied, they will not be considered usable. Terms that are too broad may need to be broken up into narrower concepts to disambiguate, often by the use of additional qualifiers. If a term is used only once, it may be wise to remove that term as an outlier and default to a more general term—but keep track of it as a possible synonym or non-preferred term. If a term is used numerous times, this establishes that the term is indeed worth indexing.

Preserve what is known as the "literary warrant" (literary warrant is discussed further later in this chapter, in Section 4.7) for each term. Literary warrant determines provenance of a term, allowing terms to be judged as viable for taxonomy use, and may provide justification for keeping a term in the thesaurus if a subject matter expert (SME) contests its inclusion. Where was the term obtained? Since the individuals creating a subject taxonomy for a topic are typically not the experts in that domain, they may need to be able to explain to a SME where a term came from and why it should be included. A taxonomist who is able to cite the sources of his or her term harvest saves time and effort when working with SMEs. Ensuing internal debates about term usage are intellectually challenging and sometimes even fun.

4.6   CHOOSING TERMS

Once a large number of potential terms have been harvested, it can be beneficial to test the raw taxonomy on real data. Generally a set of 1,000–5,000 records is substantial enough for a test, resulting in a satisfactory cross-section of the content that the thesaurus is intended to cover, but not so much that the amount of data becomes too unwieldy to evaluate. Testing a sufficient amount of data provides a basis for the work and a realistic idea of how well the work matches the customer content.

Matching an existing vocabulary against customer data is an excellent way to get a sense very quickly of whether a new or adapted thesaurus will work for a particular subject and a particular content set. If you are unsure whether to adapt a thesaurus or build one from scratch, test the prospective taxonomies and see how well they match the content at hand. Apply the terms automatically from the test thesaurus to perhaps 5,000 documents and assess the results.

Whether you test a thesaurus in construction or a candidate thesaurus, a list of terms that were not used at all may come up, terms that you may need to delete. This is one reason why a fairly substantial amount of content is necessary in testing taxonomies. Review the list of unused terms to ensure that a large part of the taxonomy is not being discarded; if this is the case, then the taxonomy in question is not adequately suited to the data. If only five or ten percent of the term candidates are discarded in the test results, the coverage hews closely to what is needed.

If you already have a taxonomy, you might need to expand it to cover a new area in a field. This could happen when, for example, a client organization adds content to its collections or gains a new subsidiary with existing files. In such cases, the taxonomy may require a new branch or area of coverage in order to index this new content. When considering an external taxonomy to expand or replace your existing taxonomy, first look at the terms currently in use and consider folding the new terms into the existing taxonomy. Draw terms from the new content that represent the kind of data covered by the taxonomy; then index the data set with the terms to see whether (1) there is already good coverage, (2) the set of potential terms needs to be expanded, or (3) a candidate thesaurus covers the new material better. Once the new terms are folded into the existing taxonomy, coverage should be adequate. Placing new terms in the existing thesaurus takes some consideration with regard to terms reflecting overlapping concepts, terms that have become outdated, and terms users are most likely to employ in a search.

One way to moderate the influx of new terms is by designating them as candidate terms, perhaps by flagging their records as they're added, or segregating them in their own branch. As jargon evolves, one might find a term never seen until very recently but currently enjoying a surge in usage. This is common with buzzwords and celebrity sound-bites. Not all candidate terms will "stick" within a field for the long term. Keeping candidate terms separate in their own branch, or using your taxonomy editing software to flag them as candidate terms, makes it easier to incorporate or discard them as needed.

Each term should be self-sufficient. Avoid using words or phrases like "*other,*" "*not elsewhere classified,*" or "*miscellaneous*" as terms, or even parts of terms. All terms in the thesaurus must be available for use in indexing your content and therefore must express genuine concepts that reflect the subject matter. No user is ever going to search a database for "other" or "miscellaneous." It is much better to have no place holders than to clutter up a taxonomy by storing junk terms.

The concept that a term expresses must be made clear by the term itself. This means that you should avoid the all-too-frequent practice of depending on inherited characteristics, that is, relying on a hierarchical relationship to lend a term meaning. For example, *diesel* should not be a narrower term of *engines* and of *fuel*. Instead, add *diesel engines* under *engines*, and *diesel fuel* under *fuel*.

Never use the same term for two distinct concepts. For example, *vectors* should not be a narrower term of both *epidemiology* and *mathematics*; *bats* should not be a narrower term of both *sports equipment* and *animals*. Instead, modify or expand the term for one or both of the concepts (*disease vectors*, *vector mathematics*; *baseball bats*).

Vague or ambiguous terms like *control* should be replaced with specific concepts like *process control* and *remote control* to serve a technology thesaurus. However, don't use terms that are too general—take into consideration the scope of the thesaurus. If the entire thesaurus is about process control, *process control* does not need to be a thesaurus term.

Don't clutter the thesaurus with terms that are not likely to be used for indexing or searching. Use the frequency counts to make this judgment—if a term produces zero hits, the user expecting to find results when searching on that term may be disappointed. If a search produces a million hits, the user will be overwhelmed with too much data that is too diverse for it to be useful.

When finalizing the terms in your taxonomy, always be sure to allow for new jargon. Any living field, even, for example, the study of the ancient Dead Sea Scrolls, continues to evolve. Given humanity's love of invention, there are always new terms coming into use, so one cannot say that the terminology is frozen for any one field. Language is a living thing. Taxonomists must account for maintenance in their thesaurus work plans; otherwise, the taxonomy will soon be rendered obsolete, people will stop using it, and all of the effort to build it will have been wasted.

Chances are high that one thesaurus will have more than one distinct set of users. These could be, for instance, bench chemists and marketers, or human resources personnel and engineers, the New York office and the London office. In the case of users from London and New York offices, or users accustomed to either marketing or engineering jargon, just because they all speak English does NOT mean they speak the same language. Sets of users may look at the same body of data, but use different terms to talk about it. To better conceptualize the needs arising from diverse user sets, then, liken it to a taxonomy or thesaurus containing both Spanish and English versions of the same terms, or correlating jargon of a particular field to common vocabulary. Consider whether it is necessary to have multiple views of terms for each user set, along with any alternatives in accommodating variant vocabularies.

An ascendant language, or *lingua franca* of sorts for the firm, should be decided upon, with terms from other languages made synonyms so that the taxonomy serves the entire corporation. Doing this is more problematic than one may believe. Say English is chosen as the ascendant language for a given firm. Which form of English? Different cognates are used to discuss individual items across cultures, settings or dialects, and though some words sound similar, they are not always spelled the same. In a multinational organization or firm, perhaps everyone speaks English, but some might speak British English, or American English, some might speak Australian English, and still others, East Indian English. When creating a thesaurus for a large multinational corporation employing both English and Spanish speakers, for example, taxonomists may find that, for the most part, differentiating between English and Spanish versions makes for an easier task than deciding ascendancy between British and American English terms.

4.7   LITERARY, USER, AND ORGANIZATIONAL WARRANT

In selecting terms for a taxonomy or thesaurus, consider their "warrant" for inclusion. Investigate how terms are used in the literature, by searchers, and how they are applied by or within organizations that utilize the vocabulary. Document term warrant in the individual term records, especially for terms for which questions regarding warrant might arise.

ANSI/NISO Z39.19-2010R identifies the kinds of warrant important for controlled vocabulary development as follows:

> *"The process of selecting terms for inclusion in controlled vocabularies involves consulting various sources of words and phrases, as well as criteria based on:*
>
> • *the natural language used to describe content objects (**literary warrant**),*

- *the language of users (**user warrant**), and*

- *the needs and priorities of the organization (**organizational warrant**)." [61]*

4.7.1   LITERARY WARRANT

ANSI/NISO Z39.19-2010R also states:

> *Assessing literary warrant involves reviewing the primary or secondary content objects that the vocabulary will be used to index, as well as consulting reference sources such as dictionaries or textbooks, and existing vocabularies for the content domain. The word or phrases chosen should match as closely as possible the prevailing usage in the domain's literature. [62]*

In the process of gathering your terms, keep track of the literary warrant for each term. It can be especially useful in the case of disagreements to be able to return to the source of a term and point out how it was used in order to justify its inclusion. Likewise, if dates are noted along with the literary warrant, one can get an idea of which terms are emergent and may therefore be worth including, even if they aren't yet used extensively.

4.7.2   USER WARRANT

Again per ANSI/NISO Z39.19, "User warrant is generally reflected by the use of terms in requests for information, on the concept or from searches on the term, by users of an information storage and retrieval system [63]." This relates to the use of search logs to harvest potential terms, but encompasses any evidence that a term is in significant use within its field. Users may refer to a concept by some shorthand or nickname more commonly than by its official term. Any terminology that is recognized in the community should be captured. The taxonomist must determine what will be the preferred term and what will be non-preferred, and stay alert for any shifting balance in preference and usage.

4.7.3   ORGANIZATIONAL WARRANT

This is really a type of user warrant. Determining organizational warrant requires identifying the form or forms of terms that are preferred by the organization or organizations that will use the controlled vocabulary.

Ultimately, it's best to use the terms the users use. They will be doing the searching. Taxonomies are built to serve the users and to help them find what they need. Being overly insistent on "proper" term usage, if it means forcing terms into forms users never use, runs counter to this goal.

4.8   TERMS AND THEIR STYLE

Many taxonomists like to view a vocabulary as a literary work, one that is more aesthetically pleasing when the style is consistent and cohesive. Consistency supports predictability when searching or browsing and makes it easier to avoid unintentional inclusion of multiple preferred terms for a single concept.

4.8.1   USE NATURAL LANGUAGE

One of the goals in creating taxonomies and thesauri is to express the concepts in natural language. This means phrasing a term in the way somebody would normally say it. We can avoid the awkward conventions of pre-coordinated, older library cataloging approaches, such as inverting word sequence ("Engines, diesel") and stringing concepts together ("Steam, combustion, and electric engines"). Instead, we have *Diesel engines*, *Steam engines*, *Combustion engines*, and *Electric engines*. With the benefit of computerized searches, we build terms according to natural ways of speaking and writing.

The biggest limiting factor with a pre-coordinated system is that, in shelving a book or other item, there is only one place on the shelf designated for that item. The classification serves merely as a guide to a single physical location for each item. This precludes related searches and searches for multiple areas within one search. To combat this limitation, some libraries actually place wooden boards with spine labels on the shelves, to provide physical cross-references for the library patrons. In other attempts to more aptly diversify searches, various library classification systems have prescribed subject headings, with detailed rules for library personnel to combine those headings in topic strings that may or may not reflect a hierarchical progression. An example is the Library of Congress Subject Headings (LCSH). The resulting strings are highly precise but rigid. Predetermined topic strings are limited in that they are neither very flexible nor search-friendly, nor do they allow for unanticipated combinations of topics of interest, and novel combinations of topics are a vital part of novel research.

As Clay Shirky has observed,

> *Let's say I need every webpage with the word "obstreperous" and "Minnesota" in it. You can't ask a cataloguer in advance to say "Well, that's going to be a useful category, we should encode that in advance." Instead, what the cataloguer is going to say is, "Obstreperous plus Minnesota! Forget it, we're not going to optimize for one-offs like that."* [64]

To make things more awkward, searches for library items have necessarily relied largely on alphabetical order, meaning that phrases are often inverted (with commas used to indicate the inversions, as in "engines, diesel"), putting the more important word first for the sake of "findability." As for searching for material within a book, there is usually a back-of-the-book index, often with the same kind of inverted phraseology.

Using computers, concept intersections can be combined at the time a search is made. Computers have made post-coordination possible since the 1960s; the Committee on Scientific and Technical Information (COSATI [65]) thesaurus, published in 1964, was the first taxonomy or thesaurus designed to take advantage of this strategy. Regardless, a heavy legacy of pre-coordination remains. The process of turning a classification system into a taxonomy or thesaurus requires changing a pre-coordinate, fragmented system to a post-coordinated conceptual approach. In developing taxonomies and thesauri that enable post-coordination of terms, the challenge comes down to stating things effectively in natural language, in terms a person would actually use to discuss a subject.

We are finding a large movement underway to render pre-coordinated classification systems of old into full thesauri; this will take great time, effort, and likely cost. The reason for this is the comparative ease of post-coordinate term creation and application in search as opposed to the much more involved process to render a classification system effective in search, not to mention the challenges of maintaining the classification or pre-coordinate systems. Despite this, some very successful conversions have recently been done, including the movement of the Physics and Astronomy Classification System (PACS [66]) to the AIP Thesaurus, sponsored by the American Institute of Physics. Another conversion is that of the Optical Classification Information System (OCIS) [67].

4.8.2   NOUNS, NOUNS, NOUNS

In modern taxonomies and thesauri, each term reflects a single concept or, less often (and mainly at the top level), a conceptual area that might be expressed in the form of two or three substantially overlapping concepts that share many subordinate concepts. Depending on the overall coverage of the vocabulary, marketing and advertising might be combined this way, or mathematics and statistical analysis, or relativity and gravitation. These single concepts or conceptual areas are best expressed in the form of nouns or noun phrases.

In your taxonomy, don't use adjectives or adverbs in isolation. "Very" by itself is obviously not a good search or indexing term. Verbs may be included in their gerund form, such as *Running* and *Fishing*. These terms function as nouns (at least in in English) and are acceptable as taxonomy and thesaurus terms. Use *Communication* instead of *Communicate*, and *Administration* rather than *Administer*, and so on.

Terms should not have initial articles. It's *Theater*, not "the theater"; it's *State*, not "the state." The exception to this rule is a proper name that includes an initial article, such as Le Mans, El Salvador, or The Hague.

4.8.3   SINGULAR VERSUS PLURAL

In general, unless a term refers to a unique item (such as singular instances, called "instances of one" in the taxonomy construction standards), it should appear in plural form. This would include items like Big Ben, which are often known by proper names. For count nouns, or names of items that one can count—*how many* telephones, *how many* desks, etc.—use the plural form. For non-count nouns, or ones that are expressed as *how much* (like cash, soil, water), the singular form is used. Count nouns are plural; non-count nouns are singular. This is mostly a matter of common sense and what "sounds" correct. If unsure which form is correct for a given noun, imagine asking about it with "how many?" in which case you use the plural form or "how much?" where you use the singular form.

There is no need to be overly rigorous about applying plural forms wherever possible. Again, use common sense and knowledge of how a word is used, and don't change water and money into waters and monies unless those forms are commonly used in the field covered by the thesaurus.

Abstract concepts that end in -tion (convention), -ism (Communism), -ity (scarcity) or a similar ending are generally expressed in singular form in speaking and writing, and so should be singular in taxonomies and thesauri. Exercise care with words whose meanings change between singular and plural like art and arts, novelty and novelties, quality and qualities, security and securities, convention and conventions, or speech and speeches.

There are some exceptions to the plural rule. In taxonomies and thesauri, anatomical terms (parts of the body, bodily systems, organs, etc.) are generally expressed in singular form. For example, in an anatomy branch, one might have *Ear*, and not *Ears*, although usually ears occur in pairs of two, with one of its narrower terms being *Middle ear*. Perhaps because of the more generic nature of the concepts being represented, *Middle ears* would seem unnatural.

As mentioned above, while unique entries are generally shown in the singular (Big Ben, Golden Gate Bridge), there will be obvious cases when the plural is necessary, especially for specific groups such as Ice Capades, and World Famous Lipizzaner Stallions.

4.8.4   CAPITALIZATION

For proper names, use capitals as appropriate. For other terms, common practice is to capitalize just the first letter of the first word unless there's a contrary conventional spelling, such as with pH. If the term is a two-word phrase, like *Electrical engineering*, capitalize only the first letter of *Electrical*.

ANSI/NISO Z39.19 suggests, but does not require, lowercasing all terms. However, the first-letter capitalization is more common in practice, and more readable. It also makes browsing a taxonomy much easier, because it's obvious where each term starts. The practice of lowercasing all terms is a holdover from the *Anglo-American Cataloguing Rules'* second edition (AACR2) standards, formerly in widespread use by library catalogers as a style guide.

Taxonomist Heather Hedden has commented on the capitalization issue:

> *The choice of initial capitalization for a thesaurus … would not be incorrect, and is probably becoming more common, just as initial capitalization is becoming more common in main entries in back-of-the-book indexes.*

A "taxonomy" implies a hierarchical classification or categorization of concepts. When we think of categories we think of labels or headings with subcategories. Headings in general tend to have initial capitalization or title capitalization. Thus, if it's a strictly hierarchical taxonomy, where all terms are interconnected into a single hierarchy or a limited number of hierarchies, then it will more likely have initial capitalization or title capitalization. Such capitalization is particularly common on the relatively smaller/less detailed taxonomies that are proliferating on websites, intranets, and content management systems. It fits in with the web design style of capitalization on headings and categories." [68]

Some taxonomies and thesauri use SOLID CAPITALIZATION throughout. However, solid capitalized terms are difficult to read and downright forbidding to skim through quickly when browsing or navigating a vocabulary. Avoiding this style is therefore recommended. The ALL CAPS style, like the all lowercase style, is a holdover from early computer times. It was used because it saved resources in the computers when storage and memory were limited. These considerations should no longer influence taxonomy style.

4.8.5   INITIALISMS AND ACRONYMS

Initialisms and acronyms are sometimes preferred terms, but only when they are better known than the spelled-out phrase. Always include the expanded name, in one form or another, even if only as a synonym of the acronym. "Laser" is more commonly used and understood than "Light amplification by stimulated emission of radiation," just as people say "AIDS" instead of "acquired immune deficiency syndrome." The preferred term is the form that is most commonly and naturally understood, with its counterpart included as a synonym for full coverage. Initialisms should be capitalized according to their conventional style. NASA and LASER are good examples of widely accepted acronyms.

4.8.6   SPELLING

Aim for consistency in use of terms that have variant forms. If your vocabulary is in English, spelling should generally follow either American English or British English conventions throughout (perhaps taking Australian English or some other variant into account), with the alternate included as a non-preferred term. Examples include *aluminum* and *aluminium*, *organization* and *organisation*, *color* and *colour*, *fiber optics* and *fibre optics*, and *call centers* and *call centres*.

In other cases in which there are two or more alternate spellings, use the spelling that is most widely recognized, or that is most likely to be favored by users of the vocabulary. Spelling preference is a matter of user warrant.

4.8.7   THE LITTLE THINGS (COMMAS, HYPHENS, APOSTROPHES, AND PARENTHESES)

In general, punctuation should be avoided in preferred terms, unless necessary for correct spelling. Depending on the software system involved, it may interfere with search. If you apply a conscious decision to exclude punctuation whenever possible, the overall terminology will be more consistent and predictable.

A comma in a term is a red flag that two or more concepts have been combined. Each term should represent only one concept, not a list of concepts. Proper names that contain commas, such as the Bureau of Alcohol, Tobacco, Firearms and Explosives, are exceptional cases and may still be unacceptable if the commas interfere with searching on a particular search platform.

Parentheses are often used to clarify the meaning of a term and can be valuable for that purpose, but this method contradicts the natural language approach. Use *Chemical binary* systems, instead of parenthetical qualifiers in terms like *Binary systems (chemistry)*. Parentheses may be lost in the computer applications used to search and store your data and should be used only when absolutely unavoidable. Instead, try to change the word order or form to eliminate the parentheses—*Chemical binary* systems, for instance. In the inverted index that forms the basic spine of search algorithms, inclusion of high ASCII characters such as parentheses, hyphens, apostrophes, and so forth can limit the searchable forms of the terms. In search, these words must be entered exactly the way they are stored, or they will not be found. They are present in the index, but not findable. To find resources indexed with "Baroque era (MUSIC)" rather than "Baroque music," searchers must know that they have to add the parentheses exactly as they appear. If they enter (MUSIC) with spaces, they will also miss the term and the associated records. Non-preferred terms or synonyms can sometimes be used to circumvent this problem.

The hyphen, another high ASCII character, can also lead to failed searches that waste time and effort. If users search for *Laser-beam* instead of *Laser beam*, they will only find the phrase exactly as they entered it. They might find *Laser* in the listing of the search results, but they will never find the *beam* independently. Organizations and content managers who insist on hyphenation are condemned to anonymity in the search and Internet world, unless they use compensating measures such as non-hyphenated synonyms or indexing rules that address both hyphenated and non-hyphenated forms. Many hyphenated words can either be separated (*dock workers*, for example) or combined into one word (*dockworkers*), so both should be considered as synonyms.

4.9   CLARITY AND CLARIFICATION OF TERM MEANINGS

In a controlled vocabulary, we strive for disambiguation, the restriction and clarification of meaning. We want the precise meaning to be clear for each term. "Reading" could mean a town in England or a language comprehension process. "Cells" could indicate biological microsystems, electrical equipment, prison housing, cellular telephones, or terrorist groups. Cell is a broadly used word and, without some additional description, we can't be sure which application is meant.

In a multidisciplinary thesaurus, a common cause of ambiguity is identical terminology used differently in different domains. One example that I have encountered several times is "Binary systems" in thesauri that cover astrophysics, chemistry, and computer engineering. In its most general sense, this phrase means the same in all three disciplines: a system with two things. However, that isn't sufficiently descriptive of its application to specific concept domains to be a useful concept for indexing content or organizing knowledge.

It is often argued that the place of a term in a hierarchy is sufficient to clarify the meaning. For a taxonomy that is used solely as a small navigation device on a website, this may be true. For indexing, keywording, or search, however, the term needs to be able to stand by itself. Although each taxonomy term automatically "inherits" the attributes of its broader terms, inheritance of broader term characteristics in a thesaurus used for keyword application is not effective. For doing that kind of indexing, each and every term would need to be represented alongside its full path in any context in which it was used. Unfortunately, this primitive "breadcrumb" approach is still widely used in web interfaces.

Parenthetical qualifiers are a simple way to disambiguate terms, as in the following examples:

Astronomy

. . Binary systems (astronomy)

Chemistry

. . Binary systems (chemistry)

Computer engineering

. . Binary systems (computer engineering)

As discussed above, this approach should be used only as a last resort. While acceptable, it is strongly discouraged. Parentheses can hide words from software.

Frequently (but not always), an expansion of the term is possible for disambiguation:

Astronomy

. . Astronomical binary systems

. . . Binary star systems

. . . Binary planet systems

Chemistry

. . Binary chemical systems

Computer engineering

. . Binary numeral system

If the thesaurus is used in conjunction with an automated or computer-assisted indexing system, an ambiguous phrase such as "binary systems" should still be included, not as a term, but as a target for the system to identify. In the content being indexed, that phrase may appear as-is in the context of one of those conceptual domains, for instance, "These stars form a binary system," and when the indexing system can take that context into account, the application of the otherwise ambiguous phrase can be resolved. If the software governing the indexing allows editors to compose the semantic rules, there might be a rule something like the:

> *Text to match*: binary system
>
> IF (AROUND "binary star" OR AROUND "binary stars" OR WITH "star" OR WITH "stars")
>
> > USE Binary star systems
>
> ENDIF
>
> IF (MENTIONS "azeotrop*" OR AROUND "mixture*" OR AROUND "alloy*" OR AROUND "suspension*" OR AROUND "colloid*" OR AROUND "heterogen*" OR AROUND "homogen*")
>
> > USE Binary chemical systems
>
> ENDIF
>
> IF (AROUND "numer*" OR MENTIONS "base 2" OR MENTIONS "base-2" OR MENTIONS "binary num*")
>
> > USE Binary numeral system
>
> ENDIF

When disambiguating terms, it's important to honor the users' use and understanding of terminology. In Chapter 2, we used the example of the term "recombination." To a geneticist, "recombination" may seem perfectly clear, in no need of further disambiguation. He or she may automatically think of genetic recombination, in which DNA strands break apart and rejoin in different ways. Even for other geneticists with a different specialty within genetics, though, "recombination" may have something to do with genetic algorithms and chromosomes. If a taxonomy covers various sciences and not just genetics, "recombination" could trigger any of the following, as described on one of the many disambiguation pages on Wikipedia:

> "**Recombination** may refer to:
>
> ○ Genetic recombination, the process by which genetic material is broken and joined to other genetic material

○ Recombination (physics), in semiconductors, the elimination of mobile charge carriers (electrons and holes)

○ Crossover (genetic algorithm), also called recombination

○ Plasma recombination, the formation of neutral atoms from the capture of free electrons by the cations in a plasma

○ Recombination (cosmology), the time at which protons and electrons formed neutral hydrogen in the timeline of the Big Bang

○ Recombination (chemistry), the opposite of dissociation" [69]

It's vital to establish what your customers and users mean by the words included in a thesaurus.

4.10   PARTS OF A TERM RECORD

Building a taxonomy or thesaurus database involves creating term records to support concepts and their relationships. The usual parts of a term record are as follows:

• a term representing the concept (the "main term" of the record);

• broader terms for that main record;

• narrower terms of that main record;

• related terms to that main record;

• synonyms, common misspellings, and other non-preferred versions that express the concept of the main record in another way or with a different text string;

• notes (definitions, scope notes, etc.); and,

• tracking information.

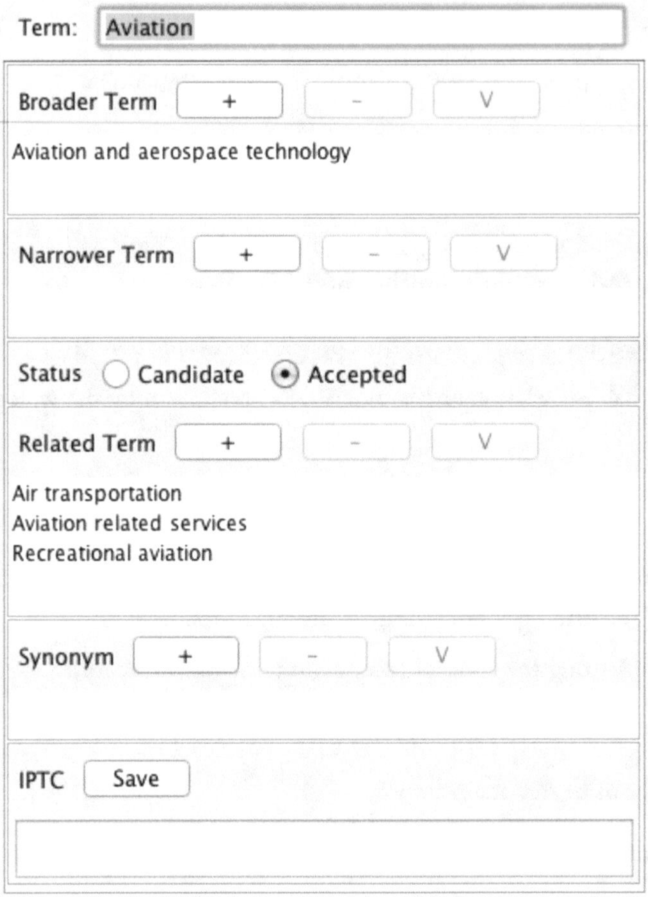

Term: Aviation

Broader Term   [+]   [–]   [V]

Aviation and aerospace technology

Narrower Term   [+]   [–]   [V]

Status ○ Candidate   ⊙ Accepted

Related Term   [+]   [–]   [V]

Air transportation
Aviation related services
Recreational aviation

Synonym   [+]   [–]   [V]

IPTC   [Save]

Figure 4.1: A Data Harmony term record.

We've already discussed several of these elements with regard to the development of hierarchical, associative, and equivalence relationships. In addition to the relationship fields, term records often include annotation ("note") fields. The most common note fields are those for scope notes and for editorial notes. There can also be fields for such things as literary warrant (or "Sources"). The taxonomy or thesaurus project administrator might consider setting up additional fields for such things as definitions, bibliographic references, and cross-references to such external resources as statutes or classification systems.

4.10.1 SCOPE NOTES, EDITORIAL NOTES, DEFINITIONS, BIBLIOGRAPHIC REFERENCES, AND CROSS-REFERENCES

Scope notes contain information about a term that you want to share with the world. They will be displayed in the public version of the thesaurus. A scope note delineates the meaning itself. It explains to the user the range of topics covered by the term. It may also include instructions for use of the term.

International thesaurus standard ISO 25964-1 [70] offers this guidance:

> _A scope note should be used to clarify the boundaries of a concept, especially when the meaning of the preferred term in ordinary discourse can be interpreted too broadly or too narrowly, or to distinguish between preferred terms that have overlapping meanings in natural language. It can also be used to provide other advice on term usage to either the indexer or the searcher. A scope note need not be a full definition but should clarify the intended use of a term within the thesaurus._

A scope note can be used to indicate or clarify meaning of a term in the context of a particular thesaurus, for its intended audience. "Stress" as a term will be different in different contexts—its meaning in civil engineering will be different from its meaning in a psychology thesaurus or in a physical therapy thesaurus; a scope note can establish and confirm the intended meaning. The scope note could also be a definition (unless the term record contains a separate field for definitions, which many thesauri do—see below). Scope notes are particularly useful for indicating any restriction in meaning, and for indicating the range of topics covered. They are often used to provide direction for indexers. In the case of pairs of terms that are often confused with each other, a scope note may suggest an alternative term.

Sometimes a scope note needs to be reciprocal; if it refers to another term, you need to post the relevant information in scope notes for both terms. Apart from that, there is no rule as to how many terms should have scope notes. Use them as needed. You might need them for only a fraction of your terms, or you might need them for almost all of the terms in your thesaurus. They don't need to be long; usually a sentence will do.

Editorial notes are similar to scope notes, but they are intended for in-house use. Editorial notes are the notes that thesaurus editors leave for themselves, saying things like, "This overlaps x, y, and z, and I don't know what to do with it." Capturing that concept when you are thinking about it is important, otherwise, you may forget your thought process when debating the warrant of that term later. When the mental dissonance happens for you, you can write it down so that someone—maybe you, maybe someone else—can find a solution when the term is reviewed later in the thesaurus creation process.

Public web displays of a thesaurus will generally not display editorial notes. Team members should use this field to document information that might be of value to other people on the taxonomy or thesaurus team of editors and compilers. For instance, an editor might indicate their reasons for choosing a particular term in preference to other possible terms.

Definitions are different from scope notes. They are something that the user should see. They often come from or could be called a glossary or dictionary. If the software supports it then these could easily pop up with a mouse over to define the term while the user is reading a full text inline tagged article or could provide substantive richness to the thesaurus as an authoritative source and dictionary for the field.

A *Bibliographic references* field is sometimes included in the taxonomy or thesaurus record as a place to add the literary warrant for the placement of a term in the spot designated in the taxonomy. When others review the taxonomy, they will understand why a term was designated in this place and within this branch and be able to trace the original works, understanding the base terminology better.

Cross-references are also known as related terms. This is a library usage of terminology and broadly used to link separate branches that are not part of the whole-part relationships of the broader-arrow term hierachy. Rather, they indicate some other kind of relationship that is potentially useful to the users of the corpus.

4.10.2 TRACKING INFORMATION

Term records sometimes include tracking information, perhaps in a History field that automatically records editorial actions, or that enables manual entry of actions taken. In addition, the field might contain term and branch import information. In general these act as log files giving a history of all the actions taken in the building of the thesaurus, who made the action and also allow a way to back out of actions taken if that avenue proves incorrect.

A *Source field* can keep track of literary warrant. Where did this term come from? Why was it used in this place? If the source information is available, it becomes clear or at least supports debate on the placement of the terms and how the taxonomist came to use or place them in a particular spot.

Some thesauri combine information from the *History* field and *Source* fields together in the *Scope Notes* field. However, I suggest keeping the term history and the source information in their separate term record fields. This separation simplifies search of these fields and enables separation of the various kinds of field entries for eventual display, as in Figure 4.1, above. It also allows use of the history field as a tracking field, while the source field can be a bibliographic reference for literary warrant.

CHAPTER 5

Building the Structure of Your Taxonomy

5.1 ORGANIZING HOW WE THINK: A BOOKSTORE EXAMPLE

All information can be organized in a variety of ways. The way that information is collected, tagged, and presented can heavily influence the way that the readership will think about it. On the other hand, a major goal in developing a structure for finding information is to match the way people already think about areas of knowledge.

Perhaps you preferred going to Borders or Hastings over Barnes & Noble, or vice versa? Online vendors such as Amazon, Barnes & Noble, and Hastings and the now-defunct Borders have different needs in their approach. They need to allow several parameters to present the desired search result to book buyers. Each of these retailers has created taxonomies for their wares, with about 25 top terms in each taxonomy. The top terms are quite broad, while their descendant terms (their narrower terms, the narrower terms of those terms, and so forth) quickly delve down into specifics.

A few years ago I went on a field trip to some bookstores to see how things were organized. Here's what I found:

Borders Books Classifications

Travel

Humor

Wellness

Food and Cooking

Religion

Psychology (which includes Magic and Erotica)

House and Garden (which includes Transportation)

Pet & Nature

History and Politics

Music and Movies

Art and Architecture (which includes Quilting and Knitting)

Romance

Science Fiction and Fantasy

Horror

Mystery and thriller

Literature (the other areas are not Literature?)

Young adult

Children's

Business and Computers (and Wedding Planning)

References

Bargain Books

New

Fiction

Newsstand

They had a shorter list in airport bookstores, but it included electronics and games instead of some of the above topics.

<u>Barnes & Noble Classifications</u>

Crafts and Hobbies (including Cookbooks and Wines)

Health and Diet (which has Nursing and Medicine)

Self Improvement (which includes Relationships, Family and Children, Pregnancy, and Childbirth, but not Diet!)

Art (which includes Gardening, Music, Rock and Roll)

Pets

Nature

Bargain

Language (including Education and Home schooling)

B&N @ School

Barnes & Noble, Jr. (including Spanish language books)

Best sellers

History (including Law)

Philosophy (including Religion & Inspiration)

Digital Photography (including Programming and Computers)

Sports

Business

Mystery

Reference (including Wedding, Photo Albums, and Jigsaw Puzzles)

Humor (including plenty of games, with a full sub-category for dice games)

There is quite a difference between the categorization systems of the two! Most people would probably have felt more comfortable in one than the other, because they understood the taxonomy used to organize one store better than the other. The same is true of the grocery store, the hardware store, and many other kinds of stores—just take a look at the signage in those stores, and then think about where you would store the items in each section. Then think about how you present information within your own organization. Is it easy and intuitive for your users to find the information items they need? The taxonomy, implied or actual, may need review and augmentation to match the way you and your users think of the information content within your organization.

5.2   OUTLINING THE STRUCTURE OF YOUR TAXONOMY

5.2.1   FIRST STEPS FOR CREATING THE TAXONOMY STRUCTURE

When you build a thesaurus, your first goal should be to achieve some degree of vocabulary control. Gather terms and organize them into a relatively uncontrolled list of terms. Then group the terms more tightly according to their conceptual relationships. Normally, only one or two people are needed for this work. In sorting a large pile of terms, it is best to have a few people dedicated to this task who can keep in mind the bigger picture of the whole conceptual area. Too many voices contributing to a conceptual area risks losing focus.

Once there is a tentative list of terms for a taxonomy-to-be, it can be a bit overwhelming, especially if they number in the thousands—a typical scientific or technical taxonomy might have 5,000–10,000 terms. How should one start dealing with them all? A good first step is to organize the information into main categories. Choose some logical main concepts, and don't be too concerned at this stage about whether or not the areas or the initial wordings are exactly how they'll end up in the finished product. This stage is for roughing things out. Use those main areas as "buckets" into which you place the more specific terms. Group similar items together for later treatment.

Many people may work on a taxonomy at one time, but team members should have carefully defined roles. One person should be assigned to create the main conceptual groupings, which will, at first, act as large categorical "bins" for sorting concepts. To start, set up those large category bins to sort concepts into. Normally, organizations already have some kind of a category list or a general outline of what their activities are, and how they perceive their content. Divisions in the outline may exist in the way of departments, product lines, or external sources. Corporations and professional associations will commonly have 16–20 broad categories they use as a general outline of their organization and its content. These lists are an excellent way to get started. If there is no set of organization-supplied categories, terms may need to be harvested from the organization's literature.

Once the general top terms are compiled, individual taxonomists can work on specific branches. Each person can take a top term or several fairly similar branches, and incorporate all of the appropriate terms into his or her territory in the taxonomy. Someone who thinks that an already placed term should be moved to a branch that he or she is working on could simply add an additional broader term relationship to that term. Allowing terms to be in more than one branch makes it easier for teams to work together on a single taxonomy. The taxonomy property of having multiple broader terms is known as *polyhierarchy*, and we will discuss this later in this chapter.

One way to significantly reduce the pile of concepts needing categorization is to remove all the authority file items first, or very early in the sorting. For our purposes, these terms are people names and place names. Names of places, names of individual people, product or service brand names, and specific objects like those we discussed in the previous chapter are all authority file candidates and should be removed at this time in the building process. These names linguistically behave differently from other terms. Weeding them out can greatly reduce the preliminary term count and contribute to early progress. The weeded-out terms can always be worked back into the hierarchy later if desired or necessary.

5.2.2   ROUGHING OUT THE STRUCTURAL RELATIONSHIPS

During this rough sorting, structural relationships among the terms will begin to emerge and other possible groupings will suggest themselves. Take advantage of those discoveries when they come. When one term is clearly a subset of another concept, make it into a narrower term. These can always be changed later. It is best not to make term relationships too complicated at the beginning, though, or there might be major untangling to do later on.

Even though you may be focusing on the hierarchical structure at this stage, flesh out the records—including scope notes, editorial notes, equivalence relationships, and synonyms—as possibilities come to mind. It's easy to forget ideas for these things after moving on to a new concept. For later additions of relationships and notes, relying entirely on your memory can be a losing proposition. Adding the information to the notes and tracking information fields now will be an advantage later in the process.

In looking at terms that fit in the same general area, some terms are closely related conceptually, but not hierarchically. A taxonomist may want users to be aware of a particular term when looking at a conceptually similar term in a different area of the taxonomy, such as *Hiccups* under

Medical conditions, and *Hiccup cures* under *Treatments*. These conceptual links should be expressed in a thesaurus as *associative relationships* between *related terms*.

Synonyms and quasi-synonyms are also sorted at this stage, as well as in later stages. Quasi-synonyms are those terms or concepts that are similar but not identical. Such terms share a general conceptual sphere. Group synonyms and quasi- or near-synonyms together; if one single term covers the general concept, decide whether the others should be included as narrower terms or synonyms. A good rule of thumb is that if non-preferred synonyms are not exact synonyms, they should be more specific in meaning than the main term. Otherwise, the resulting indexing might be inaccurate. For instance, *spiders* and *arachnids* are often thought of as the same kind of animal, as spiders constitute a large proportion of arachnid species. While all spiders are arachnids, not all arachnids are spiders; ticks, mites, and scorpions are also arachnids. Suppose that a biological taxonomy contains the term *Spiders*, and that *Arachnids* is a non-preferred synonym of *Spiders*. Suppose further that in the content being indexed using that taxonomy, a journal article mentioning arachnids focuses on ticks and mites, and completely ignores spiders. With a fully automated indexing system, the article will be indexed as being about spiders.

The use of terms that exist only for term grouping purposes is not recommended. Thesaurus standards do allow the use of non-indexing terms for term grouping purposes, and sometimes this is necessary. However, searchers tend to become frustrated when they see a term that is exactly what they want, only to learn that nothing is indexed with that term. This is why a term for the purpose of grouping—a "node label" [71]—should be identified as such with a different type font, or by being enclosed in brackets or parentheses.

There may be conceptual gaps in the taxonomy term collection, gaps that become evident only after work on organizing the taxonomy has begun. Watch for topical areas that are within the scope of the taxonomy, but that are missing from it. Search logs may reveal areas that users are interested in but that are not yet covered in the taxonomy. Often, concept or term gaps are elusive. As in any editing task, it can be easier to spot problems like this after putting a little distance between oneself and the project.

When a term seems to fit well in more than one hierarchy, use multiple broader terms, or *polyhierarchical relationships*. Add these as soon as they present themselves. They can always be edited later in the process, if necessary. It is easier to evaluate and possibly remove them later than it is to remember the options you had in mind after being away from that part of the taxonomy for a while. We will discuss *polyhierarchy* later in this chapter.

The same idea holds with associative term relationships: add them as soon as they come to mind.

5.2.3   THE ALL-AND-SOME TEST

Once the rough sorting is completed, the product is an alphabetical list of terms with a few relationships added. Term records are next. Analyze each of them using the hierarchy as the point of entry to the term clusters. To test whether a concept should be a narrower term or a related term, use the "all-and-some" test.

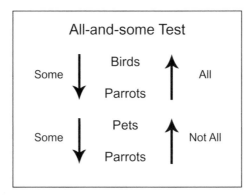

Figure 5.1: The all-and-some test.

The illustration above shows that *Parrots* is a suitable narrower term of *Birds*, but not of *Pets*. **All** *Parrots* are *Birds*, and some *Birds* are *Pets*. *Parrots* fits within the *Birds* category. In addition, **some** *Parrots* are *Pets*, but **not all** *Parrots* are *Pets*.

    ✓   ALL *Parrots* are *Birds*

    ✗   NOT ALL *Parrots* are *Pets*

    ✗   NOT ALL *Pets* are *Birds*

All parrots are birds, but not all birds are parrots; therefore, *Parrots* is a subset of *Birds*, and a suitable narrower term. *Parrots* may be considered *Pets* in some contexts, but not all *Parrots* are always considered *Pets*. Some are live in the wild, so it is not true that all *Parrots* are *Pets*, and therefore *Parrots* should *not* be a narrower term of *Pets*. Likewise, not all *Pets* are *Birds*—other *Pets* can be *Cats*, *Dogs*, or *Fish*. 100 percent of a concept must fit within the broader term. If one of the terms does not neatly fit completely and entirely underneath the other term, then it can have an associative relationship with the other term, and may be indicated as a *related* term. Related terms demonstrate that a relationship of some kind exists between two concepts, but not one that would qualify them as broader or narrower terms of each other. *Parrots* and *Pets* should be made related terms.

5.2.4   CRAFTING THE HIERARCHICAL STRUCTURE

The top terms you create at first should be thought of as tentative, and are likely to change during the creation process.

Ideally, there should ultimately be between five and twenty top terms. Twenty terms fit easily in most screen displays of a taxonomy hierarchy; more than that might not fit well. Too many terms at any level is too big to be helpful to users of a thesaurus. Unless it is an authority file list, each level should have about the same number of terms under each successively narrower term. Limit the number of terms at the same level in each branch to twenty terms where practical. If there are more than twenty terms, see if one of them could serve as a broader term for some of the other terms at that level, keeping in mind the all-and-some rule described above.

Avoid grouping compound terms together simply because they have a word in common. For example, *Pest control* and *Process control* do not belong together under the broader term *Control*. The common word in compound terms is often vague or ambiguous, and therefore useless for grouping terms or for indexing. Moreover, the terms having the word in common may belong to entirely different subject areas.

In the next section, we will discuss a couple of options for approaching how you will craft the hierarchy structure.

5.3   BOTTOM UP OR TOP DOWN?

Bottom up and top down are two opposite, but completely compatible, approaches to developing hierarchical structure. The bottom-up approach might be described as starting with the content, whereas the top-down approach might be described as starting with the basic hierarchical structure.

On page 91 of the printed version of the ANSI/NISO Z39.19-2010R [72] controlled vocabulary standard, the two approaches are explained as follows:

(a) Top Down—The broadest terms are identified first and then narrower terms are selected to reach the desired level of specificity. The necessary hierarchical structures and relationships are created as the work proceeds.

(b) Bottom Up—This case frequently occurs when lists of terms have been derived from a corpus of content objects and are then to be incorporated in a controlled vocabulary. As in the case above, the necessary hierarchical structures and relationships are created as the work proceeds, but starting from the terms having the narrowest scope and moving to the more generic ones.

Eminent taxonomist Jessica Milstead explains the process of thesaurus construction largely in terms of following either "The Top-Down Method" or "The Bottom-Up Method." F. Wilfrid Lancaster describes the top-down approach (which he also calls the "deductive" approach) as something of an ivory tower brainstorming approach, often involving committees and not involving investigation of the relevant literature. He finds that the approach has two major problems.

1. "It is difficult to think of all the categories or hierarchies that will be needed."

2. "The characteristic used to subdivide a genus may not lead to a classification that best meets needs of users. For example, the class 'toys' could be subdivided by material, by colour, by age of intended audience, by method of locomotion, and so on. For a toy manufacturer, one of these characteristics (perhaps age) may be much more important than some of the others." [73]

Lancaster favors the bottom-up approach:

"The empirical (i.e., bottom-up or "inductive") approach to thesaurus construction is the opposite extreme and it tends to be much more reliable. Terms occurring in the field are collected from various sources and a category or hierarchy of terms is formed only if it appears to be important or useful. For example, a subdivision of toys by colour (blue toys, red toys), while theoretically possible, may have no significance to the toy manufacturer for whom the thesaurus is created." [74]

Well-known information management consultant Leonard Will has a somewhat different view of how to use the two approaches:

"I don't think that there is only one "logical" way of building a hierarchical structure of concepts. You can do it "top down", by starting with broad categories and populating them with terms to represent narrower and narrower concepts."

You can also do it "bottom up", by collecting terms (from previous schemes and user suggestions, from the literature, from queries and so on), sorting these concepts into facets [by which he means major categories] and then grouping these into hierarchies."

In practice I generally use a combination of both these approaches." [75]

Bottom-up is the most common because most often a list of terms already exists. Once a taxonomy is completed, a new branch may be added as a speculative activity, in which case it is better to use the top-down approach. Bottom-up gives the best results when there is already a body of knowledge from which to draw. I suggest that you use the top-down approach at the top term level selection, but only after determining the major term topic categories, and then switch to a more bottom-up method. This combination seems to be the most natural and efficient overall approach.

5.4   HIERARCHICAL LEVELS

The more specific or specialized the area covered by the thesaurus, or the more specific the knowledge domain being dealt with, the more specific and deeper the thesaurus can be. When building a thesaurus for a fairly narrow photonics and imaging engineering database, for instance, it is relatively easy to provide great depth of coverage. On the other hand, with a broad multidisciplinary collection covering a wider variety of science, for example, all of physics, coverage of any one discipline tends to be less specific and detailed.

To cover any field adequately, be mindful of what degree of depth, clarity, and specificity will be sufficient to cover the content as the user thinks of it. Covering a multidisciplinary database with many documents on a varied and broader range of topics is challenging, because the user queries vary widely. The graduate student searching to support dissertation topics requires high precision and great specificity, while an elementary school student working on a science fair project requires a much more general representation of the subject area. Getting the right balance for the user base and properly representing as many facets of knowledge as possible can have a strong impact on the success of research using the resulting thesaurus.

The application of a taxonomy in the web environment needs to follow different rules than a thesaurus built to index a collection to the "most specific level," as recommended by ANSI/NISO Z39.14-1997 (R2009), "Guidelines for Abstracts," and the complementary "Guidelines for Indexing and Related Information Retrieval Devices," by James D. Anderson, NISO Technical Report 2 (NISO-TR02-1997). Information architects will recommend that taxonomies—particularly corporate taxonomies—should be limited to three levels, because of web users' assumed reluctance to click through any more than three levels when browsing. This three-level limitation is more prevalent in consumer taxonomies. It is probably not applicable to government and professional association taxonomies associated with research databases, where it is in the nature and experience of the intended users to dig for information. Nevertheless, it is still a prevailing and popular notion that users will give up after three clicks [76]. To satisfy this restriction, up-posting in taxonomies is suggested. For web displays, roll up or up-post deeper terms to each successive broader term until only two or three levels are left. In this way, all of the terms deeper in the branch (*narrower terms*) function as synonyms of their broader terms. This allows for excellent returns in search based on thorough indexing for the display to quickly return, within a few clicks, a useful answer for the searcher. Your thesaurus may have many more levels—be much deeper—and you will use those deeper layers for the actual tagging, but the terms are "rolled up" or "up-posted" to the next higher or broader term until there are only three levels for display. For example, your indexing taxonomy might go to five levels to be specific enough for the content you are covering in the taxonomy. However, you might decide that you only want to use the top three levels on the website. The rule of thumb on web implementations is three clicks, so a deeper thesaurus is only appropriate for some sections for the web presentation where you know the user is willing to click through to five levels.

However, to accommodate your content, you must have the deeper indexing options, especially for automatic indexing and to follow the NISO Z39.14 indexing standard. So the solution is to up-post your terms as quasi-synonyms to the next highest level. This gives you the benefit of accurate indexing while supporting the impatient web user.

All taxonomies, and most computer-based thesauri, are hierarchical in structure. This allows for creating consistency of depth for different subject areas in a well-constructed vocabulary. A taxonomy should be roughly the same depth throughout. This depth will vary significantly from vocabulary to vocabulary, as the thesauri available are drastically different in sizes. Some of them go down only three levels, and some of them go to twenty levels or more. Consistency in depth leads to balance in coverage, as well as ease and predictability in browsing and navigating the vocabulary.

5.5   POSSIBILITIES FOR HIERARCHICAL RELATIONSHIPS

As we've seen in earlier chapters, the defining characteristic of taxonomies is the presence of hierarchical relationships. Information specialists recognize several types of hierarchical relationships. These types may offer ideas for adding terms as you develop the hierarchical structure.

I suggest that in general, you try to keep the narrower terms of any given term in the same type of hierarchical relationship. For instance, if one of the narrower terms of *Proteins* names a specific kind of protein, you might consider doing likewise with its sibling terms to keep the nature of the terms parallel. While this approach is not a hard-and-fast rule, and is not always practical to do, it can enable easier browsing of the taxonomy.

Generic relationship—This relationship identifies the link between a class and its members or species. The generic relationship is generally called the *Broader term/Narrower term* relationship. This relationship is most clearly demonstrated in traditional biological taxonomy of organisms, because of its well-established and well-known groupings of phyla, classes, orders, genera, species, and so forth; e.g., *Rodents* and NT *Squirrels*.

This is sometimes referred to as an "isA" relationship, in reference to the kind of relationship that the narrower term has to its broader term. Using our example from the "all-and-some" rule discussion above, a parrot "isA" bird.

Instance relationship—This is another variation on the "isA" relationship. The difference between this kind of relationship and the generic relationship type is that in an instance relationship, the narrower term represents a single instance in the category identified by its broader term. In other words, the narrower term is a class of one. An example of this relationship follows:

Seas

NT Baltic Sea

NT Caspian Sea

NT Mediterranean Sea

In the NISO/ANSI standard, these narrower terms are called Narrower Term Instances, or NTI. Some software uses "NTI" to indicate the narrower terms in this kind of relationship, although this differentiation is of limited usefulness for most applications.

French cathedrals

NTI Chartres Cathedral

NTI Rheims Cathedral

NTI Rouen Cathedral

NT Gothic cathedrals

The instance relationship is a way to accommodate specific people, places, and things in the most appropriate place in the hierarchy if they are not placed into authority lists.

Whole-part relationship—This relationship is just what the name implies. As described in ANSI/NISO Z39.19, "This relationship covers situations in which one concept is inherently included in another, regardless of context, so that the terms can be organized into logical hierarchies, with the whole treated as a broader term." [77]

There are three types of term combinations that are often described as having whole-part relationships:

Systems and organs of the body

Geographic locations

Hierarchical organizational, corporate, social, or political structures.

Many other types of terms can be in whole-part relationships, as well. In a sense, a sub-discipline of an academic discipline could be considered to have a whole-part relationship with the broader discipline, although this could also be viewed as a generic relationship.

Body systems and organs

Ear → Middle ear

Remember that, as we discussed in the previous chapter, taxonomy terms for body systems and organs are customarily given in singular form, rather than the usual plural form. This seems more natural, probably because of the more generic nature of the concepts being represented. Here, the actual concept is "the middle ear" in an anatomical sense, rather than the collective world of people's and creatures' middle ears.

Geographic locations

New Mexico → Bernalillo County → Albuquerque

Hierarchical, social, etc. structures

Cricket leagues → Cricket league divisions → Cricket teams → Cricket players

Historical or geochronological time spans

Mesozoic era

→ Triassic period

→ Jurassic period

→ Cretaceous period

Fields of study

Geology → Physical geology

The abbreviations BTP (broader term (partitive)) and NTP (narrower term (partitive)) are sometimes used to identify the terms of a whole-part relationship.

Polyhierarchical relationships—These are also referred to as "multiple broader terms." ANSI/NISO Z39.19-2010R explains: "Some concepts belong, on logical grounds, to more than one category. They are then said to possess polyhierarchical relationships. . . . These relationships may be represented using the BTG and BTP notation." [78]

Nurses

. . Nurse administrators

Health administrators

. . Nurse administrators

Careers

. . Accounting

Finance

. . Accounting

Polyhierarchy is a relatively recent development in the world of classification. It takes advantage of computer capabilities that can go beyond the physical limitations of the physical library or museum collection. It is also necessary for adequate indexing of digital objects in large databases.

5.6   ADDING ASSOCIATIVE RELATIONSHIPS

Provide cross-hierarchy relationships and enrich the information that your term records provide to users by entering existing thesaurus terms in the *Related Term* field. In a term record for *Quiche*, you could add *Vegetarian foods* as a related term, by adding it in the Related Term field or possibly by selecting the term from the overall display of terms, depending on your software. You wouldn't want to make *Quiche* a narrower term of *Vegetarian foods*; a quick thought exercise will bring to mind some counter-examples like *Ham quiche* or *Quiche Lorraine* that violate the all-and-some rule.

You can relate terms freely, as long as the concepts they represent are genuinely related in some way and if you don't add so many related terms that it's difficult for users to single out the most useful ones. Related term pairs can even be opposites. Often people add opposites like height and depth, broad and narrow, tall and short, because you never know if people will be looking for how deep an ocean is or how tall a mountain is. When building an ontology, such relationships become even more important. In a physics taxonomy, you might have the terms "Matter" and "Antimatter," for example, or in a taxonomy of movies you might have the terms "Zombies" and "Living people."

5.7   ADDING EQUIVALENCE RELATIONSHIPS

Terms in an equivalence relationship refer to the same concept or sometimes a roughly equivalent concept. They are usually synonyms. As has already been discussed, there should be only one indexing term or preferred term in your thesaurus for any given concept. You can and should include synonyms of those terms in your thesaurus as synonyms. We do that using equivalence relationships. The synonyms that aren't "preferred terms" are "non-preferred terms" in the same term record. Your taxonomy software instructions will indicate how to add non-preferred terms to term records, and this action will establish an equivalence relationship between the preferred term and each non-preferred term.

Equivalence relationships are created in different ways, depending on the kind of thesaurus you are building. In a thesaurus for general use, you might use *Grapes* as a preferred term, and *Vitis* as an equivalent non-preferred term. In a scientific thesaurus, on the other hand, you might use Vitis as the preferred term, and *Grapes* as the corresponding non-preferred term. The same is true for scientific versus trade names. You might use *Motrin*, which is a trade name, or *ibuprofen*, which is the generic name. You might need to put both in a thesaurus, but the one that should be the preferred term will depend on who uses the thesaurus.

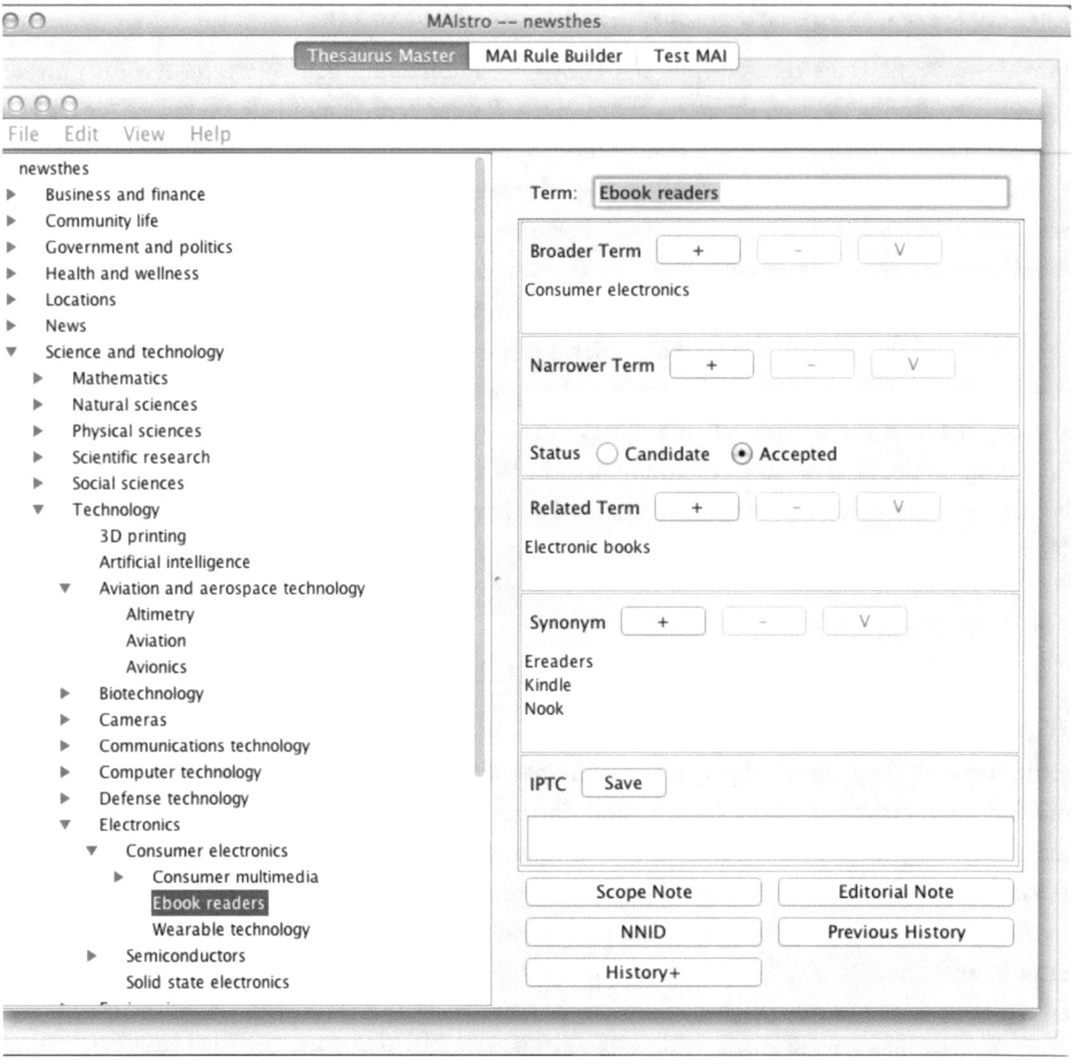

Figure 5.2: A term in Thesaurus Master, showing a broader term, related term, and synonyms. Note the empty fields for narrower terms and a user-specific identification code.

We also need to know if we will use the standard names or the slang names—*Sci fi* versus *Science fiction*, or *Hippos* versus *Hippopotamuses* versus *Hippotami*. Normally, taxonomists use the standard names, but slang names are acceptable, especially if they are more widely used by their user community than the standard names.

In different cultures, even in what is essentially the same language, different terminology is often used. *Home care for the aging population* is a recognized phrase in the U.S., but in the U. K. it is *Domiciliary care*. I have read the Harry Potter series by J.K. Rowling in both British and American English, and even the titles are different—*Harry Potter and the Sorcerer's Stone* in the U.S. is *Harry Potter and the Philosopher's Stone* in Britain, for example. Another consideration is emerging concepts whose terminology has not yet stabilized; for example "Web logs" are now called "Blogs." There are outdated terms such as *ice boxes*, now called *refrigerators*, for example.

There are also lexical variants, which are variant spellings, such as the terms *Moslems* and *Muslims*. There are words whose usage has changed, but the older literature will still contain the terms. For example, *Gipsies* and *Gypsies* were both widely used at one time but are now considered pejorative, the more generally acceptable wording is *Romani people*. For an effective search and indexing thesaurus, all variants should be included as synonyms. The choice of which variants of ethnic and religious names to use should reflect the respective peoples' own preferences if possible, and reflect what the searching user will use to identify them. This exercise will take you down interesting trains of thought about the need for political correctness and incorrectness as dual necessities in taxonomic work. Some are quite uncomfortable. On the one hand, you have the euphemisms that develop and need to be accounted for as synonyms, or even preferred terms. On the other hand, you have the clearly offensive terms that also need to be included for proper tagging (for example, take the use of the N word in Mark Twain's fiction). As a taxonomist, you really need to be insensitive to terms regarding inclusion, but highly sensitive when designating preferred terms that might be displayed.

Quasi-synonyms are pairings such as *Urban areas* versus *Cities*, or *Gifted people* versus *Geniuses*. While the meanings of these terms may not be exactly the same, they are conceptually similar enough that they may occupy the same space in the thesaurus.

There are many options and computer format tables for the transliteration of non-roman alphabetic languages such as Arabic and Tamil. The Arabic word commonly translated as *Caliph*, for instance, can be transliterated *Halifah*, *Kalifa*, *Khalifah*, *Khalyfah*, or *Kaliifat*. This leads to great variation in the presentation of the name of any particular concept or group. At this stage in your taxonomy construction project, consider including all of them.

When working with a source that includes any of the languages that incorporate non-Roman character sets, such as Mandarin Chinese, Korean, Japanese kanji, Russian Cyrillic, Greek, and many others, the challenge may be even greater. There are many different ways to spell a term and its conceptual equivalents. And, of course, the accepted spelling may vary.

Americans tend to go for ever more abbreviated spelling, while the British like to keep their long spellings. Consider the American *Catalogs* and the British *Catalogues*. And then there's *Weblog*, coined in December 1997 by Ohioan/New Mexican Jorn Barger [79], and shortened to Blog less than two years later by Californian Peter Merholz [80].

As for abbreviations, I recommend capturing both the abbreviation and the full form. Some articles might discuss *ECGs* or *EKGs* or *electrocardiograms*. We need to put all three forms into the same term record, with one form as the preferred term because over time, different users will use all three forms. In a medical thesaurus, the preferred term would probably be the fully spelled-out form.

Antonyms are another great resource for building out the taxonomy. Using each term and its opposite concept strengthens the thesaurus. They can also be made into equivalent terms: *Height* and *Depth* might effectively be the same concept for some purposes; so might *Literacy* and *Illiteracy*. If you add one, you might as well add the other one, either as an additional, and perhaps related, preferred term or, if you are looking to save space and not worried about the granularity of your thesaurus, as an equivalent term.

The standard software designations for equivalent term pairs are "USE FOR" for non-preferred terms and "USE" for the preferred terms: *Automobiles* USE FOR *Cars*; *Cars* USE *Automobiles*. They, along with the "See" and "See also" references, seem to be library science artifacts and not useful in the thesaurus, taxonomy, and other controlled vocabulary constructions. They are counter-intuitive and confusing. For the most part, you can let your software deal with them. I use the preferred and non-preferred term syntax instead.

5.8   A DAY IN THE LIFE OF A TAXONOMIST: WORKING WITH TAXONOMY STRUCTURE

What is a day in the life of a taxonomist like? What kinds of discussions do they have, and what kinds of things do they think about? Throughout the course of a large thesaurus creation or revision project, discussions are usually at the term level and decisions are made term-by-term, in-house. The taxonomy is submitted to the customer for periodic review, usually after the taxonomy has been fleshed out hierarchically.

The following is taken from a taxonomist's communication regarding a thesaurus revision in progress.

Ceramics: Move under *Materials*? Cut other industrial materials loose from *Materials* branch?

Materials: This is now under *Materials science*. Perhaps it should be restored to top term status, especially inasmuch as it has industrial materials as narrower terms.

Computer terms: Should probably be consolidated somehow. The current computer terms at the top are *Computer engineering*, *Computer networks*, *Computer programming*, *Computer science*, and *Computer software*. We are not sure where to draw the line between computer engineering and computer science. Computer networks defy simple categorization, as they encompass hardware setups and areas like the Internet and ad hoc networks.

Software engineering: Seems like it should be on a level with *Computer engineering*. However, it is currently under *Computer applications*, which is under *Applications* (one more of those broad ambiguities mentioned above).

Errors: Does not seem to belong at the top; corresponded regarding possible placement. Have different meanings in different contexts, especially in *Statistics* as compared to everything else. Currently have its narrower terms disassociated from it, distributed among *Data communication systems/Coding errors* (where most of the error terms ended up), *Measurement*, and *Statistics*. Perhaps it could be folded into *Mathematical techniques*? (This might accommodate all the "errors" terms in a rough way. Should they be restored to BT Errors?)

Heat transfer, Mass transfer: Kept these as top terms for classification code correlation purposes. Perhaps their true home is *Physics*?

Industry, Industrial plants: In view of the nature of the terms under *Industrial plants* (many of which may eventually be correlated with their corresponding classification codes), perhaps it should be restored to the top level? Alternatively, could the terms under *Industry* and under *Industrial plants* be moved to broader terms specific to particular industries? (A related issue: Should the various industries be represented at the top level?)

Power generation: Identified this earlier as a gap in the top terms. It does exist in the thesaurus, but it is badly misplaced. The root cause seems to be a mix-up between *Energy conversion* and *Energy conservation*. *Energy conversion* is *Power generation's* broader term; perhaps it should be a top term (with *Power generation* under it). Currently, *Energy conversion* is under *Energy management* in the classification codes. One of the terms under *Energy management* in the classification codes is *Energy conservation*. In the thesaurus, *Energy conservation* (along with *Soil conservation* and *Water conservation*) is under *Conservation*, which is under *Environmental engineering*.

Problem solving: A problem term. *Management? Math? Cognition?*

Protection: Has had all its narrower terms disassociated and moved elsewhere, because they didn't have a lot in common. (Also, most of those terms did not previously have a hierarchical relationship with the terms representing the areas in which they belonged.) Basically, the narrower terms divided into *People protection* and *Protection of property*. The former suggest *Safety engineering*, and the latter suggest *Materials science*. What to do with the term? Delete it? It is of little meaning by itself.

Tuning: At the top, only because a broader term has not been decided on. *Electrical engineering*, perhaps?

The day progresses along this line, with the taxonomist dealing with tangles of terms, where to place them, and how to define them in the context of the customer context and document collection.

5.9   THE USER'S PERSPECTIVE

Classifying an organization along its conceptual lines for taxonomy would be a wonderful methodology. Most of the time, though, there is an existing culture within the organization that must be honored and applied in the interest of retaining the organization's self-image. The taxonomy must reflect the way they think of themselves. It is also true that a new perspective, especially a taxonomic one, can provide an alternative view of the organization that may be closer to the current truth than the historically evolved self-image. Valuable insights can be drawn from examining how a firm organizes itself around, or counter to, its data. In order to ensure implementation of your taxonomy, it is best to capitalize on the users' organizational culture. Use what your users will use. Then expand on it to ensure that the taxonomy will accommodate growth and development within and external to the organization and the content. A content-aware taxonomy is crucial to good implementation.

CHAPTER 6

Evaluation and Maintenance

You have what could be considered a first draft of your taxonomy after you have finished the following activities as covered in the previous chapter:

1. incorporated all the selected terms in your term lists into the taxonomy,

2. arranged the terms into what you believe to be a logical hierarchical structure, and

3. for a thesaurus, added associative and equivalence relationships that seem potentially useful.

Now the taxonomy is ready for the evaluation stage.

6.1   EDITORIAL REVIEW

This may seem obvious, but proofread your taxonomy. Verify the spelling of unfamiliar or difficult terms. Misspellings not only look bad, but also can thwart thesaurus searches, rule base searches, indexing, and document searches. Then have someone else proof it. Sometimes you can no longer see your own errors because you have spent so much time looking at the work so closely.

Check once more for balanced coverage of the subject area, watching out for possible gaps and unnecessary duplication. "Orphan terms" are those without any hierarchical relationships to other terms. They are terms that are on their own as narrower terms under a given broader term. "Orphan terms" are sometimes referred to as "Only child(ren)," although "Orphan term" here is the preferred term. Try not to leave any orphan terms in your taxonomy. Inclusion of these kinds of terms can easily happen in the course of taxonomy development, but in the evaluation stage they should be discovered and resolved.

The presence of an orphan term suggests that there may a conceptual gap. If the specificity of that term was appropriate, there may well be parallel concepts of similar specificity that should be represented. If *Digital processing systems* is in the thesaurus as the only narrower term of *Signal processing systems*, consider adding *Analog signal processing* and *Automated signal processing*.

Digital processing systems as an only child:

Signal processing systems

. . Digital processing systems

and with siblings added:

Signal processing systems

. . Analog signal processing

. . Automated signal processing

. . Digital processing systems

When surveying your thesaurus, take advantage of your software's capability to expand and collapse the visual display of the thesaurus structure. This capability enables you to skim through terms at the same level, and to "drill down" to focus on terms at various levels in a single branch.

If possible, also have someone who is familiar with thesaurus best practices and standards do a thorough review.

6.2   USE TESTING

The potential use of a taxonomy generally takes one or both of two forms: (1) indexing records—bibliographic records, articles, journals, reports, and so forth—using terms in the thesaurus; and (2) searching. Both of these two major uses should be tested at first, and then tested again for maintenance of the taxonomy.

We mentioned testing the taxonomy against your content early in the process. Do it throughout the process, and especially at the end of the project. This gives you the means to prove that the thesaurus does indeed accurately represent your content. Run all the records through the thesaurus; look for over- and under-indexed records—records that come back with too many or too few indexing terms. Also run a frequency count again to ensure that the terms in the thesaurus are all used (but not over- or under-used) to index the content.

Running your records through the thesaurus indicates that you are programmatically matching the records or content to the thesaurus terms. When we do this, we first do the automatic indexing and then look at the results in several ways. First is to add all the times a term was applied somewhere in the indexing process. Was it used thousands of times (over-indexing, needs to be more specific) or few times—even zero times (under–indexing, needs to be a different preferred term or is not appropriate concept of that taxonomy). Sometimes an outside subject matter expert will insist on a term but when you run the data, that term turns out to be too broad or too narrow to be effective. This gives us the first look at the effectiveness of the thesaurus.

The second thing is to look at the records themselves. Are there some with too many terms? Are there some with no terms? We need to ensure that all records have terms in the thesaurus that will cover their conceptual content. We also need to be certain that there are not too many terms applied to a single article. It would be a very unusual work that would have too many appropriate terms. The balance is important for providing even retrieval for the user. We want to support precision, getting exactly what they want, recall, getting all of the material on that topic and relevance to their query, by using the right terms to describe the topic.

If this is achieved through the indexing process, then the search process will return similar results and the users will find an effective delivery mechanism for the information they seek.

Finally, look at the indexing of the individual articles. Are the terms applied actually reflective of the content? We take a random sample and evaluate based on these statistics: the number of HITS, or application of terms appropriate to the articles; the number of MISSES—the number of times concepts that should have been applied to the article from the taxonomy and were not; and the amount of NOISE—when inappropriate terms were applied to the articles. In doing this we can calculate an accuracy number for the taxonomy we have created. Some of the terms need to have a complex rule built so they will index appropriately. Some terms need to be restated to match the actual content in the corpus. Some terms should be removed—there is no content that represents that concept in the data itself.

A thesaurus that has not been tested against the client content is not useable or reliable.

6.3   EXTERNAL REVIEW

In addition to your internal editorial review and testing against the actual content, it is very important to get external review of the taxonomy. Once you've gotten the taxonomy together, you've organized the hierarchies, you've built the term records, and you've tested it on the target content, it is time to go and get an outside review. You want to get both user-level review and a review by subject matter experts. The two groups will use the thesaurus differently and think about it differently.

Before you start asking people for feedback, you should realize that most of the feedback you get will probably be based on the taxonomic or hierarchical view. You already should feel confident that the terms that you have built the term records around are indeed the proper terms—you have verified that they are in use and appropriate to describe content. Where they are placed in the hierarchy is a matter of perspective and use. At this stage, the terms' inherent meanings are not under discussion (there is an exception to this rule—when considering the conceptual inheritance of a term, the meaning(s) of terms may dictate hierarchical placement). You are using the terms to index; they are the facts of the vocabulary, so to speak. You use the hierarchy to navigate, display, and handle the terms; that is the interpretation. People can agree on facts, yet find radically different interpretations. The same is true of a taxonomy. You can change it easily to reflect different perspectives. Remain willing to do that in the face of the subject matter experts' opinions or the customer's wishes, after you have heard from everyone doing reviews.

6.3.1   USER LEVEL REVIEW

User level review is best done in a controlled environment. There are two kinds of users: (1) searchers who will be using a search system to find things they are interested in, and (2) editors or indexers who will be applying the taxonomy terms to the content prior to publication. The searcher or end user testing is discussed in a section on implementation of search in Volume 3. The editorial testing must be done prior to full launch of the taxonomy within the production environment. The editorial team must be comfortable with the taxonomy coverage and understand its importance to the eventual end user and the creation of the products of the organization. Once this groundwork is laid, they are the best team to ensure that the terms are truly appropriate to the content presented. They may review the test set of records to ensure that the terms are hits, misses, or noise and provide that feedback. They may also review the full thesaurus, giving expert user understanding of the content to be indexed and the tool to be used. We often find that they are initially threatened by the new system, even though it is there to aid them and the creation of their final products. Some caution is warranted and therefore full understanding of the process is particularly important in getting their review. As with the subject matter experts, it is best to ask them to do and review with a guideline and understanding of the work.

6.3.2   SUBJECT MATTER EXPERTS

Subject matter experts (SMEs) are an extraordinary resource. They have trained for many years, developing high levels of expertise. They know their areas very well. They may continue to have a broad perspective on the field in general as well as their own area of expertise. They understand the nuances of terms and concepts in their field and are willing to share them. When doing a taxonomy review, you need to treat the SMEs with respect.

Subject matter experts need to be used in creation of a good taxonomy—proceeding without their knowledge means you will miss some important detailed knowledge. However, they also need to be managed carefully. It is not a good idea to bring them into the process before you yourself have gained enough knowledge of the subject and the terms to truly understand their input and defend your term placements.

Be sure you have actual documents or articles to back up your placement of the terms. The literary warrant, as we discussed in previous chapters, of the terms' usage is critical. "I found the term used this way in this article" is much more effective than "I think it should be used this way." Use the terms the way the experts in the field use them, and have your literary warrant at hand to show examples. Flexibility is important here, as SMEs may differ from their colleagues in the way they use certain terms—when you present your literary warrant to John Q. SME, he may indicate that Bob Q. SME is going about his research all wrong! If you talk to Bob Q., he might very well say that John Q. is the one who is mistaken. For now, remain open to both sides of the issue and reserve final judgment for later.

When you have several experts, you will need to balance their comments and find common ground in their term use. This is very helpful for disambiguating the finer points of the taxonomy terms. Get them to agree, if you can, and then use the results. Balance the subject expertise they bring with your own expertise as a taxonomist. Ideally, you will teach them how the taxonomy works, and they will teach you what the terms mean and how they are used. In the end, they will become advocates for the taxonomy, urging others to make use of it. When you and the SMEs can work together, the results will usually be excellent and broadly applicable.

Our experience shows that one fruitful way to work with subject matter experts is to have one of the taxonomists sit with the subject matter experts to obtain their feedback on one or more specified branches of a taxonomy. The taxonomist can implement the changes immediately, surfacing any problems raised by, for example, changing the placement of a term. At the same time, the taxonomist hears the perspective of each expert firsthand. The taxonomist can jot down the SME's insights as notes or make changes immediately.

My experience has been that if the main taxonomist spends one or two hours talking with the subject matter expert, it will take about eight hours to fold in the results of the discussion with that SME. When you get SME feedback, expect to spend several times the amount of time spent with an SME working their comments into the taxonomy—rearranging the hierarchy, adding scope notes, adding term relationships and non-preferred terms, and so on.

Sometimes it is easier for SMEs to give their feedback on a spreadsheet or other means of display. Any form for the feedback is good, but personal interaction is the most effective, because you can immediately verify what the SME meant. In an interview situation, you can get instant clarification if you don't understand the feedback.

Here's a list of when and how to use subject matter experts.

- For evaluating candidate terms

- For determining which of several synonyms to use as the preferred term

- When you can't determine what a term means, or where it fits conceptually

- For periodic review of taxonomy progress, to maintain focus on the core areas with proper attention paid to peripheral topics

- For final review of the taxonomy

There are times when you should not seek SME input.

- Early in the taxonomy development process

- For the initial top term selections

- For day-to-day taxonomy development work

- When specific subject matter expert input is clearly contrary to taxonomy standards or best practices (Yes, this happens.)

6.3.3   THE DANGERS OF SUBJECT EXPERTS AND SILO THINKING

Above we talk about the wonderful and many benefits of SME review. However, SME review is a double-edged sword because these experts tend to have a definite idea of what their portion of the field looks like. But do they know the whole field? They may be looking at the field from only their own narrow perspective. Do they have a good and broad overview of how everyone will approach the subject? Often they do not. If their Ph.D. took them down ever-narrowing paths into a highly specific subtopic, they might not have a good perception of where the field is overall.

Subject matter experts are masters *in their own field*. They are not experts in taxonomy or thesaurus construction. Their specialized expertise can lead them to focus so strongly on their own very specific area of expertise, or "silo," as some information professionals call it, that they lose perspective on the vocabulary as a whole.

As people gain more expertise in a field, they tend think very narrowly about that field instead of giving a really broad orientation to it. As far as they are concerned, their area will be the most important one—after all, it is what they study! Their influence has the potential to bias the entire taxonomy. Therefore, the taxonomist must balance their input with the opinions of other experts.

One real-life (and very typical) example I've seen is one expert's placement of *Finance* under *Agriculture*. This would be acceptable in a taxonomy that's only about agriculture, and for which the associated content is limited to agricultural topics. The actual concept in that case, though, might be *Agricultural finance* or something similar. A taxonomist might want to take advantage of the subject matter expert's input to capture an important concept with a new term, but not necessarily the exact term that the SME suggests.

6.3.4   HOW TO DISAGREE WITH AN EXPERT

There are three important things to observe when you disagree with an expert.

- Disagree respectfully.

- Have the facts to back up your point of view.

- If possible, recommend an alternative that takes the SME's suggestion into consideration.

Here's a real-life example of a carefully worded disagreement: "Re: *Ising model*. With all due respect for [a well-known thesaurus], I think *Magnetism* is too limiting as a BT (but is good as an RT). Per Wolfram Research: The *Ising model* has more recently been used to model *phase separation in binary alloys and spin glasses.* In biology, it can model *neural networks*, *flocking birds*, or *beating heart cells*. It can also be applied in *sociology*."

Facts to back up your point of view can be your literary warrant. If you have literary warrant that includes multiple instances of the use of a term in the same manner but in different documents or publications, that gives your argument more weight than just one occurrence. You don't need to spend a lot of time locating literary warrant for every term, but for particularly disputed terms, finding a few additional instances might help.

As you created your hierarchy and fleshed out term records, there may have been one—or more—terms that you opted not to use. Take another look at those, to see if one of them will be a better fit for the term in question.

6.3.5   TAXONOMY REVIEW GUIDELINES FOR SUBJECT MATTER EXPERTS

When I request SME input, I provide the SMEs with the set of guidelines shown below.

> **Things to keep in mind when suggesting changes—moves, deletions, additions, synonyms, relationships, etc.**
>
> *Hierarchical relationships are based on specific conceptual links.*
>
> Broader/narrower term relationships (also known as parent/child terms, BTs/NTs) define the hierarchical structure of the thesaurus. For one term to be the child term of another, it should be a subset, part, or instance/example of the parent term. Generally, other ways in which concepts are significant to each other constitute associative relationships (Related terms, RTs).
>
> *Terms should make their meanings clear by their wording and phrasing.*
>
> Wherever possible, terms should be expressed in clear, natural language. If there are more technical expressions or jargon for a term, those should be included as synonyms.
>
> *Fill in gaps.*
>
> In developing a taxonomy, the goal is to achieve balance and the appropriate degree of comprehensiveness in subject matter coverage. If there are essential/important concepts (or even whole areas) that you find have been missed, mention them. If common variants of terms have been left out that should be included as synonyms, please suggest them.
>
> *Point out errors, and recommend fixes.*

Don't just apply these guidelines to suggestions of your own, but keep them in mind while reviewing the terms already in place. If you find any terms that are misworded, misplaced, or otherwise not in line with these standards, please let the taxonomy editors know.

6.3.6 THE VALUABLE PARTNERSHIP BETWEEN TAXONOMISTS AND SUBJECT MATTER EXPERTS

As taxonomists we bring an area of expertise of our own. We have a way of sorting the SMEs' language into a structure. We are not the subject matter experts ourselves, but we are experts in something else—word and concept organization. We reach out to the SMEs to help us with the taxonomy. We need them to explain the science and how things fit together. They need us to help explain the organization. The partnership with the SMEs leads to richer expression of the taxonomy concepts and more accurate reflection of the database contents to be indexed with the taxonomy.

6.4 I COLLECTED, I SORTED, I STRUCTURED, I TESTED, … WHEN WILL IT BE FINISHED?

(Excerpts from a *TaxoDiary* blog posting by Dr. Jay Ven Eman, November 7, 2011)

"Is it final? Finally! I recall Rex Harrison playing Pope Julius II, shouting up to Charlton Heston as Michelangelo, something like, "When will it be finished?" To which Michelangelo-Heston replied enigmatically, "When I'm done!" Michelangelo spent most of five years (1477–1480) on his back painting the Sistine Chapel. The Pope's impatience was not without justification as he was financing the project while trying to recapture former Papal territories filched by the Borgias.

The same question is often asked of taxonomy and thesaurus development: "When will it be done?" The answer is, "Never!" which is less enigmatic than Heston's reply, but not very palatable to those Popes trying to pay the bills while the Borgias (read: Barbarians) are at the gates. How do you know when your taxonomy building efforts are done is a legitimate question and concern. The tart reply "Never!" really means your taxonomy needs to be kept up to date. But you still need to know the criteria for releasing it for widespread use. At some point you will want to actually use it to classify and label content and to use it to guide navigation. …

While your thesaurus is never done—and should be never done—there comes a time when you can—when you must—start using it. Let your audience see it and then embrace the feedback. It will only get better. Michelangelo finally had the scaffolding removed and people marveled then and still do today. (A tourist tip: When visiting the Sistine Chapel you can save a lot of time by going in the back door!)"

Figure 6.1: The Sistine Chapel north and east walls.

6.5   MAINTAINING YOUR THESAURUS

Once you get into the maintenance phase, you have to be able to edit and otherwise change any part of the term records. You might change the name of the term itself. You could change the term or add non-preferred synonyms. You might want to delete or add a relationship. Of course, you'll want to add new terms. You might want to move the branches around. All of these things are part of routine taxonomy maintenance.

As concepts and technologies change and advance, so does terminology. Once the thesaurus is in use, it is crucial that it be kept up to date with the literature it covers. On a regular—I suggest at least monthly—basis, you should follow several avenues of maintenance to ensure currency.

6.5.1   KEEP A SCHEDULE

Review your thesaurus on a regular basis to determine what updates you should make.

- Examine the keywords that are suggested by editors but don't appear in the thesaurus. Some of those keywords may indicate terms that should be added to the thesaurus.

- Review the search logs to be sure you are keeping up with emerging terms, concepts, and technology. Search logs show the interaction of the user with the content by capturing the queries they make of the system.

- Add new terms for evolving concepts as needed. Before adding a new term, always check for existing terms that cover the concept or that could or should be modified.

- When searching the thesaurus, use single words rather than phrases, and use character strings truncated by a wildcard character (usually an asterisk, depending on your software), rather than full words with specific endings. Searching for *econ** instead of just *economics* or *planet** instead of just *planetary* will show you all the places that some form of each searched word is in use.

- Truncation is a commonly used method to cut a word to its root or just a section of the word. It is also called stemming or lemmatization. In all cases it can be either right or left truncation. Right truncation is straightforward for a computing point of view. The word is simply chopped off, and the searchable inverted index or alphabetic look-up list would then include the stemmed and perhaps the entire word forms. Left truncation is much more difficult to implement. Cutting a word on the front end or the left side involves creating a much larger look-up list or table and leads to many erroneously and unforeseen results in the search presentation.

- Term deletion is no problem when you are into the building phase of a taxonomy. During creation, terms have a fluid existence. However, once the terms have been applied to a large corpus of text, they are embedded in the searchable or archival database. They may exist in the XML of the entire collection. When a term is deleted from the taxonomy, it is no longer applied to the newer text. But the older material still uses that term. Before deleting a term, consider the potential effects in relation to documents that have already been indexed with the term, and in relation to future searches. Best practice is to either (1) add a new synonym for the term—more current conceptual term usage and retire the other term to the equivalence tables or (2) reindex all records using the revised term base.

6.5.2   COMMON MISTAKES

It is easy for one or more of these faults to creep into your taxonomy or thesaurus in the course of routine maintenance. Watch out for them.

- Overly vague terms

- Lack of balance in terms

- Gaps in coverage

- Too many top terms

- Not enough levels ("flat" structure)

- Same term (essentially) in two places in thesaurus, but with different style (*Milky Way galaxy/Milky Way Galaxy*; *Bird houses/Birdhouses*)

- Two or more synonymous terms (*Biochemistry/Biological chemistry*) as regular thesaurus terms

- Too many terms at any one level within a branch

- Inappropriate BT-NT relationships

- Term placed in an entirely incorrect/inappropriate location in thesaurus hierarchy because the meaning or relationship is misunderstood or not well thought out

- Term is misplaced in the taxonomy because of shared word or morpheme

- Spelling errors (more common than you might think!)

- *Other* or *Miscellaneous* as terms or as the beginning of terms

- Terms that don't have any meaning, or whose meaning isn't clear, apart from their hierarchical context

- Abbreviations or lingo that are meaningless (to the user)

After a thorough evaluation and putting in place your maintenance schedule and process, you are ready to move on to integrating your taxonomy into the workflow of the organization. This is covered in Book 3 of this series.

SOME RULES OF THUMB

Phrase a term in the way somebody would normally say it.

Each term should reflect a single concept.

On average, there should be about 1.5 non-preferred terms for each preferred term.

Don't use adjectives or adverbs in isolation.

Terms should not have initial articles.

For count nouns—*how many*—use the plural form.

For non-count nouns—*how much*—use the singular form.

Abstract concepts that end in -tion, -ism, -ity, etc., are generally expressed in singular form.

Anatomical terms (parts of the body, bodily systems, organs, etc.) are generally expressed in singular form.

Unique entries are generally shown in the singular (Big Ben, Golden Gate Bridge).

For proper names, use capitals as appropriate.

Initialisms should be capitalized according to their conventional style, such as with NASA and LASER.

Use the spelling that is most widely recognized by your user community.

Punctuation should be avoided in preferred terms.

Avoid hyphens.

Avoid using parentheses.

Hierarchy will not solve an ambiguity problem. Use another method.

Evalauate your taxonomy or thesaurus on at least a monthly basis.

CHAPTER 7

Standards and Taxonomies

We've discussed what it takes to make the components of a digital information model work. The glue that makes them work together is standards.

The entire idea of using a controlled vocabulary, in whatever form and by whatever name—thesaurus, ontology, taxonomy, authority file, pick list, attribute table, knowledge organization system (KOS)—is to standardize the nomenclature that an organization uses to tag, keyword, add descriptors, add controlled vocabulary, add subject headings, add content tags, semantic indexing, etc., to their content so that it can be found, searched, and retrieved.

There are several controlled vocabulary standards, as well as networking protocols, that have an impact on taxonomy implementation. There are also standards having to do with markup, metadata, and data modeling that impact thesaurus construction and implementation.

7.1 WHAT DO WE CALL THESE THINGS?

Perhaps a guide to the standard(s) would be helpful in resolving some of the confusion about what to call these things. Following is a list of the standards to which we refer frequently. They come from two ISO committees (TC 46 and TC 37), ANSI/NISO, BSI, the W3C, the US Library of Congress, IFLA, and others.

1. ANSI/NISO Z39.19 [81]—Guidelines for the Construction, Format, and Management of Monolingual Controlled Vocabularies (2010)

2. ISO 25964 [82]—Thesauri and interoperability with other vocabularies, Part 1: Thesauri for information retrieval (2010); and Part 2: Interoperability with other vocabularies (2013)

3. OWL Web Ontology Language [83]

4. SKOS [84]—Simple Knowledge Organization System

5. ISO 704:2009 [85]—Terminology work—Principles and methods

6. ISO/NP 860:2007 [86]—Terminology work—Harmonization of concepts and terms

7. ISO/CD 1087-1 [87]—Terminology work—Vocabulary—Part 1: Theory and application

8. ISO/TR 22134:2007 [88]—Practical guidelines for socioterminology

9. ISO/TR 24156:2008 [89]—Guidelines for using UML notation in terminology work

10. ISO 29383:2010 [90]—Terminology policies — Development and implementation

A review of the list of content standards above reveals that the preponderance of them are NISO/ISO standards.

7.2   SO WHO ARE THESE STANDARDS GUYS AND WHY SHOULD WE LISTEN TO THEM, ANYWAY?

ISO is the International Organization for Standardization [91], based in Geneva, Switzerland. ("ISO" is not an acronym; it's a short form based on the Greek word isos [92].) ISO has members representing the national standards organizations of 163 nations; each of those nations has one vote on each standard. Because the standards world is very complex, it covers everything from the size of the threads on a light bulb to the way that electrical sockets work to how we format and categorize words into a taxonomy.

ANSI, the American National Standards Institute [93], sets USA standards and also votes on behalf of the United States at ISO. NISO, the National Information Standards Organization [94], is part of ANSI. ANSI has designated NISO to represent the USA's input on information and documentation standards to ISO. NISO is one of the 30 or so maintenance agencies for standards in the U.S. NISO is responsible for library and information standards. Standards identified with "Z39" are from NISO. ANSI/NISO Z39.19, *Guidelines for the Construction, Format, and Management of Monolingual Controlled Vocabularies*, is the official thesaurus and taxonomy standard for the United States. I highly recommend having a copy of the Z39.19 standard in your library.

ISO has an extraordinarily large coverage area and so has created a multitude of Technical Committees [95], or TCs. The standards having to do with thesauri and terminologies are concentrated in TC 46 [96] and TC 37 [97]. TC 37 deals primarily with terminology and other language and content resources, and TC 46 deals with information and documentation. Each TC has subcommittees (SCs) in order to bring broad input and expertise to bear on specific standards. The TC 46 is the ISO counterpart of NISO.

7.3   CREATING STANDARDS

The process for the creation of a standard through these organizations is a lengthy process, since it requires all the voting members to come to a consensus on each proposed standard. Votes can be "no with comment", and each of those must be resolved before the standard can become official. It can take two years or more for this process to complete, but this is one way of creating a standard.

Two years is too long for some in the web community—the pace of change in the Internet Age is often much faster. Organizations like the W3C [98, 99]—the World Wide Web Consortium—were founded to move the standards process along more expeditiously. The W3C adopted a different model for standards advancement. They instruct a working group to draft a Recommendation, which is a specification or set of guidelines that has been endorsed by W3C members and the director. A Recommendation from the W3C is essentially equivalent to standard from the other organizations we mentioned above. The W3C publishes the Recommendation on the web with a Request for Comment (RFC). Some people begin implementing as soon as the draft comes out of the working group. These people are known as early implementers or early adopters. For example, when XML 1.0 was published by W3C, it seemed like a sensible approach and we began using it in my company immediately for software development. An RFC can go through several iterations and is a very open process. That is, everyone can see the comments and yet still move forward quickly—in Internet time.

In Chapter 3, we talked about SGML, HTML, and XML, and those were all first created as standards via the W3C. The TCP/IP protocols (Transmission Control Protocol/Internet Protocol [100]) also came out of the W3C's work, and progressed quickly into widespread use by early adopters.

Some organizations, like national libraries, have long shared resources and set standards for information sharing, either physically or digitally. The U.S. Library of Congress has a number of standards which they create, oversee, and maintain [101] for metadata and transfer of information between libraries and publishers. Recently, the International Federation for Library Associations and Institutions (IFLA) [102] has also gotten active in standards, for everything from public libraries to namespaces and the Functional Requirements for Bibliographic Records [103]. (FRBR)

Everywhere we turn, standardization is in progress. Keeping up with the changes and ensuring that products and services are compatible will continue to be important and must be a constant awareness activity for good providers. The value of speaking the same language is increasing as vocabularies become more prevalent and more likely to be shared and reused. Interoperability is essential, and standards make it possible.

One of the nice things about standards is that there are so many to choose from! As I mentioned above, for those of us who work with the control of vocabularies there are two main standards. ANSI/NISO Z39.19-2010R and ISO 25964 are the principal standards. In addition, there are many others that have been built for specific purposes and applications within specific environments. Since this book is in English, the standards referenced are in English, although there are several other notable standards that I suggest reading, especially the French and German standards (French NF Z47-100: *Rules for the establishment of thesauri in the French language* [104], Germans (OENORM DIN 1463-1: *Guidelines for the establishment and development of thesauri; monolingual thesauri* [105]). The list is ever changing, but those in current use at the time of publication are listed at the end of this chapter.

The organizational and control standards from ISO/NISO that we have mentioned above are ones that directly affect our work, and for our purposes here we focus our attention on those that cover taxonomy implementation. In the storage, retrieval, and preservation standards associated with field formatting and tagging, there are additional standards that cover how and where the thesaurus terms will be placed into one or more fields in a database. When we work with unstructured data (that is data without field formatting or XML tags applied), adding metadata, we are adding structure to undifferentiated text and making it much richer. In order to put metadata into a specific field, we need to know which field to use. There are standards for that, and therefore we need to be aware of the standards and how they work so that we will know where to put the data.

There are also some classification standards and some publishing standards. Particularly in our case, we observe the subject indexing standards. There was a standard for "How to index", but it ran into trouble because it focused on the way back-of-a-book and other pre-coordinate (see Chapter 5) indexing is done. This is not the same way that you do indexing for online databases, and trying to wrap all of the necessary components into a single standard didn't work. James Anderson from Rutgers University [106] did a masterful job in trying to put the two methodologies in the same standard, but they are very different and the unified approach finally sank. People couldn't agree.

Dr. Anderson's work has been published as a NISO technical report (not an official standard), *Guidelines for Indexes and Related Information Retrieval Devices*, NISO TR02-1997 [107]. Someday the dust will settle and perhaps the standards bodies will take it up again and make two official standards.

Figure 7.1: Alvin Weinberg.

Controlled vocabulary standards have been around at least since the 1960s in one form or another. A major landmark in this area was the set of guidelines created in 1967 by the Committee on Scientific and Technical Information (COSATI [108]) of the Federal Council on Science and Technology [109] when they developed TEST [110]—the Thesaurus of Engineering and Scientific Terms. A group of forward thinkers convened at Oak Ridge National Laboratory at the request of nuclear physicist Alvin Weinberg [111] (1915–2006), who was reacting to the launch of Sputnik by the Soviets and felt a strong need to build a better information infrastructure in the United States. The result of this meeting was the *Guidelines for the Development of Information Retrieval Thesauri*, guidelines for what we now know as the Internet, along with associated options for search and retrieval. They spurred the development of computer architecture, with a focus on text based objects, which was then and remains now quite different from the transaction processing focus that pervades the world of computer science. TEST is the first thesaurus created with the goal of computer-based information retrieval. It was widely adapted and shared. Organizations that took advantage of TEST and augmented it for their journal and report collections included DuPont, Engineering Information, Inc. (Ei), the Institute of Electrical and Electronics Engineers (IEEE), the National Aeronautics and Space Administration (NAS), and the Defense Technical Information Center (DTIC), among others.

Not long after this, the French wrote a thesaurus standard that is amazingly similar (*NF Z47-100: Rules for the establishment of thesauri in the French language* [112]), as did the Germans (OENORM DIN 1463-1: Guidelines for the establishment and development of thesauri; monolingual thesauri [113]), as did the U.S. standards organization. The first edition of the American standard, the Z39.19, based on the COSATI guidelines, was published in 1974.

In 1985 and 1986, ISO published ISO 2788 and ISO 5964, standards for monolingual thesauri and for multilingual thesauri, respectively. Later, between 2005 and 2008, the British Standards Institute (BSI) released the five parts of the standard BS 8723, *Structured Vocabularies for Information Retrieval*. You will notice that the most recent version of Z39.19 was originally published in 2005, the same year that the BSI released the first part of BS 8723. There were parts of the standards where the British Standard said one thing and the U.S. standard said the exact opposite, which was very frustrating. Those of us who are in the information community wanted an international standard in which there were no conflicting directions to the user. Resolving those discrepancies began the slow march toward a compatible and technologically updated ISO standard.

The most recent ISO standard for controlled vocabularies, the two-part ISO 25964, is a significant departure and upgrade from the previous standards. The original intention was that it would be very much like the British standard. In fact, the author of Parts 1 and 2 of BS 8723, Stella Dextre Clark [114], took the lead in writing it. Parts 1–4 of the British standard have been completely re-written and are folded into Part 1 of the ISO 25964 standard [115].

Part 2 of the ISO 25964 standard, which significantly expands on the British standard, covers interoperability. The coverage includes interoperability among standards but also with search systems. It is a really fine piece of work [116].

7.4   AN ABBREVIATED GUIDE TO THE STANDARDS

Below is a partial list of taxonomy-related standards.

ANSI/NISO Z39.19-R2010 [Approved in 2005, and reaffirmed without change in 2010]

Guidelines for the Construction, Format, and Management of Monolingual Controlled Vocabularies

Presents guidelines and conventions for the contents, display, construction, testing, maintenance, and management of monolingual controlled vocabularies. It focuses on controlled vocabularies that are used for the representation of content objects in knowledge organization systems including lists, synonym rings, taxonomies, and thesauri.

ISO 25964-1:2011

Thesauri and Interoperability with other Vocabularies: Part 1: Thesauri for Information Retrieval

Gives recommendations for the development and maintenance of thesauri intended for information retrieval applications, whether monolingual or multilingual. It is applicable to vocabularies used for retrieving information from all types of information resources, irrespective of the media used (text, sound, still or moving image, physical object or multimedia) including knowledge bases and portals, bibliographic databases, text, museum, or multimedia collections, and the items within them [117].

This part of ISO 25964 also provides a data model and recommended format for the import and export of thesaurus data.

ISO 25964-2:2013

Thesauri and Interoperability with other Vocabularies: Part 2: Thesauri and Interoperability with other Vocabularies

Today's thesauri are mostly electronic tools, having moved on from the paper-based era when thesaurus standards were first developed. They are built and maintained with the support of software and need to integrate with other software, such as search engines and content management systems. (For example, data from the thesaurus database might need to be presented in combination with the number of postings found by a search application.) Whereas in the past thesauri were designed for information professionals trained in indexing and searching, today there is a demand for vocabularies that untrained users will find to be intuitive, and for vocabularies that enable inferencing by machines.

ISO 25964 makes the transition that is needed in order to be compatible with the world of electronic information management. However, this part of ISO 25964 retains the assumption that human intellect is usually involved in the selection of indexing terms and in the selection of search terms. If both the indexer and the searcher are guided to choose the same term for the same concept, then relevant documents will be retrieved. This is the main principle underlying thesaurus design, even though a thesaurus may also be applied in situations where computers make the choices.

Efficient exchange of data is a vital component of thesaurus management and exploitation. This part of ISO 25964 therefore includes recommendations for exchange formats and protocols. Adoption of these will facilitate interoperability between thesaurus management systems and other computer applications, such as indexing and retrieval systems, that will utilize the data.

This part of ISO 25964 covers development and maintenance of thesauri rather than how to use them in indexing. Where multilingual issues and examples are addressed, efforts have been made to cover as wide a selection of languages as possible, consistent with clarity and comprehensibility.

Thesauri are typically used in post-coordinate retrieval systems, but may also be applied to hierarchical directories, pre-coordinate indexes and classification systems. Increasingly, thesaurus applications need to mesh with others, such as automatic categorization schemes, free-text search systems, etc. ISO 25964-2 will address additional types of structured vocabulary (such as classification schemes, name authority lists, ontologies, etc.) and give recommendations to enable interoperation of the vocabularies at all stages of the information storage and retrieval process.

ISO 704:2009

Terminology Work - Principles and Methods

Establishes the basic principles and methods for preparing and compiling terminologies both inside and outside the framework of standardization, and describes the links between objects, concepts, and their terminological representations. It also establishes general principles governing the formation of designations and the formulation of definitions. Full and complete understanding of these principles requires some background knowledge of terminology work. The principles are general in nature and this document is applicable to terminology work in scientific, technological, industrial, administrative, and other fields of knowledge [118].

ISO 860:2007

Terminology Work: Harmonization of Concepts and Terms

Specifies a methodological approach to the harmonization of concepts, concept systems, definitions and terms. It applies to the development of harmonized terminologies, at either the national or international level, in either a monolingual or a multilingual context.

In spite of all the efforts made to coordinate terminologies as they develop, it is inevitable that overlapping and inconsistent terminologies will continue to be used because documents and policies are produced in different contexts. Differences between concepts and misleading similarities at the designation level create barriers to communication. Concepts and terms develop differently in individual languages and language communities, depending on professional, technical, scientific, social, economic, linguistic, cultural, or other factors. Harmonization is, therefore, desirable because:

- differences between concepts do not necessarily become apparent at the designation level;

- similarity at the designation level does not necessarily mean that the concepts behind the designations are identical; and

- mistakes occur when a single concept is designated by two synonyms which by error are considered to designate two different concepts.

Harmonization starts at the concept level and continues at the term level. It is an integral part of standardization.

ISO 1087-1:2000 [Slated for revision]

Terminology Work: Vocabulary: Part 1: Theory and Application

The main purpose of this international terminology standard is to provide a systemic description of the concepts in the field of terminology and to clarify the use of the terms in this field. The compilation of this vocabulary provided a forum for analyzing, discussing and coordinating key concepts found in ISO/TC 37 standards. This International Standard is addressed to not only standardizers and terminologists, but to anyone involved in terminology work, as well as to the users of terminologies.

The terms in this International Standard are listed in a systematic order under a number of general headings.

The layout follows the directions given in ISO 10241. Thus, the elements of an entry appear in the following order:

- entry number

- preferred term(s)

- admitted term(s)

- deprecated term(s)

- definition

- example(s) | reference to another entry in bold face followed by entry number in brackets, when it is first mentioned

- note(s)

Entry number, preferred term and definition are the mandatory elements of each entry. Other elements appear only when appropriate.

The notation used in the notes throughout this International Standard is as follows:

- concepts are indicated by single quotes;

- designations (terms or appellations) are in italics;

  NOTE: The use of italics facilitates the understanding of this standard, but it is not in conformity with ISO 10241.

- characteristics are underlined; and

- types of characteristics are doubly underlined.

The alphabetical index includes preferred and admitted terms.

Annex A contains concept diagrams which represent the relations among the concepts defined in the vocabulary.

It should be noted that the examples of terms are specific to the English language in the English version and to the French language in the French version.

ISO 10241-1:2011 (Revises ISO 10241:1992)

Terminological Entries in Standards: Part 1: General Requirements and Examples of Presentation

To ensure that communication in a particular domain is effective and that difficulties in understanding are minimized, it is essential that the various participants use the same concepts and concept representations. The standardization of terms and definitions is thus fundamental to all standardization activities.

Even when the immediate results of standardization are monolingual terminological entries, to facilitate communication in science and technology, cross-cultural communication, the exchange of goods and services, as well as the formulation of policies and strategies at national, regional, and international levels, terminology work has to be multilingual in its approach. Even in countries with only one official national language, standardizing bodies sometimes prepare multilingual terminological entries for the purposes mentioned above.

Standardizing bodies often choose to standardize terms and definitions and to publish the result as terminological entries in standards. This part of ISO 10241 has been prepared to provide rules for the drafting and structuring of such terminological entries in standards; it is based on the principles and methods given in ISO 704.

Within ISO, the standardization of principles and methods for the preparation of terminological data primarily referring to concepts and terms is under the responsibility of ISO/TC 37.

ISO/TC 12 and IEC/TC 25 are responsible for the symbols for quantities and units. These symbols are often derived from terms, and often look like an abbreviated form of the term, although the symbols have an additional communicative function. They are the subject of the ISO 80000, IEC 80000, and IEC 60027 standards.

ISO/TC 145 is responsible within ISO for the overall coordination of standardization in the field of graphical symbols, with the exception of those for technical product documentation. This responsibility includes:

- the standardization of graphical symbols, colours and shapes, whenever these elements form part of the message that a symbol is intended to convey (e.g., a safety sign), and

- the establishment of principles for the preparation, coordination and application of graphical symbols.

Although the work of ISO/TC 145 excludes the standardization of letters, numerals, syntactic signs, mathematical signs and symbols as well as symbols for quantities and units, such elements may be used as components of a graphical symbol.

ISO 10241-2:2012

Terminological Entries in Standards: Part 2: Adoption of Standardized Terminological Entries

Addresses the introduction of standardized terminological entries into other cultural and linguistic environments, and in particular the adoption of internationally standardized terminological entries by regional and national standardizing bodies. It establishes principles and guidelines for dealing with the key issues to be considered in this process. It also provides examples of, and solutions to, problems that occur when the adopting standardizing body adopts internationally standardized terminological entries, aligns the concept systems of the adopting standardizing body with internationally standardized concept systems, and prepares standardized terminological entries as additions or supplements to internationally standardized terminological entries.

ISO 12616:2002 (Reviewed and confirmed in 2012)

Translation-Oriented Terminography

Provides guidelines to enable translators and translation support staff to record, maintain and quickly and easily retrieve terminographic information in connection with translation work.

Translators have always had a need to record terminological information for later use. Translators dealing with specialized texts face an increasing need to record and retrieve terminological information, as it saves time and allows them to work more efficiently. Experience has shown that terminography facilitates translation by enabling translators:

- to record and systematize terminology,

- to use terminology consistently over time, and

- to deal more efficiently with multiple languages.

By recording terminological information systematically, translators can enhance their performance, improve text quality and increase productivity. An organized collection of terminological information makes it possible for translators to keep track of, and reuse, their expertise, and facilitates cooperation between individuals or teams of translators.

ISO 12620:2009

Terminology and Other Language and Content Resources: Specification of Data Categories and Management of a Data Category Registry for Language Resources

Provides guidelines concerning constraints related to the implementation of a Data Category Registry (DCR) applicable to all types of language resources, for example, terminological, lexicographical, corpus-based, machine translation, etc. It specifies mechanisms for creating, selecting and maintaining data categories, as well as an interchange format for representing them.

ISO/TR 22134:2007

Practical Guidelines for Socioterminology

Proposes guidelines for socioterminology principles, methods, and vocabularies. *Socioterminology* Terminology standardization has always been the prerogative of experts in terminology, the latter dealing exclusively with technolects. In this context, the principles, method and vocabularies drawn up by terminologists are not always suitable for the speakers' communities which are heterogeneous. This situation does not lend itself to permitting mutual understanding between these linguistic communities.

Socioterminology which is linked to localization facilitates communication between different socioprofessional groups. It studies terminologies, placing them within the social context where the concepts appear, are defined and are named. It unites the specialized concepts with a community of speakers. In this way, socioterminology enables terminological practices to be adapted to the target languages and linguistic communities addressed by the linguistic work.

The drafting of practical guidelines for socioterminology is an attempt to match what is said and what is done in the daily life of speakers. Although the methodological principles drawn up by planning terminologists seem to have a relatively universal spread, the ensuing practices on the other hand, will be adapted to the targeted linguistic communities. It is in this context that this Technical Report will be used for the interpretation and usage of the other TC 37 documents within the perspective of cultural and linguistic diversity and, therefore, within the meaning of terminology planning practice on the world scale.

ISO 29383:2010

Terminology Policies: Development and Implementation

Provides policy makers in governments, administration, non-profit, and commercial organizations with guidelines and a methodology for the development and implementation of a comprehensive policy or strategy concerning the planning and management of terminology. Defines key concepts and describes scenarios and environments which may require different kinds of terminology policies. It also places terminology policies in the broader context of institutional strategic frameworks.

All of these standards are excellent reading and should be a part of all taxonomists' reference libraries. I think the U.S. standard, ANSI/NISO Z39.19-2005, also known as Z39.19-R2010 (NISO reaffirmed its validity in 2010), is the easiest to read. If you are going to stay up late and want a nice standard to read, that would be the one I'd recommend.

Glossary

AACR, AACR2

See Anglo-American Cataloguing Rules.

Accuracy (in search results)

The quality of search results, as measured by any of a variety of metrics or determined by subjective factors.

All-and-some rule, All-and-some test

A method for evaluating the validity of broader term–narrower term relationships. *Some* of whatever a broader term represents should be represented by each of its narrower terms, and *all* of what a narrower term represents should fit within the concept represented by a broader term.

***Amarakosha* (also *Namalinganushasana*)**

An ancient Indian thesaurus written in Sanskrit. It reportedly served as an inspiration for *Roget's Thesaurus*.

American National Standards Institute (ANSI)

The official standards organization for the United States.

Anglo-American Cataloguing Rules (AACR, AACR2)

A set of guidelines (or the publication containing those guidelines) used by library catalogers as their style guide. It has been published jointly by the American Library Association, the Canadian Library Association, and the U.K.'s Chartered Institute of Library and Information Professionals. In 2010, AACR2 (the 2nd edition of AACR) was superseded by the Resource Description and Access (RDA) cataloging standard.

ANSI/NISO Z39.19 (Z39.19)

An American National Standard developed by the National Information Standards Organization (NISO), and approved July 25, 2005, by the American National Standards Institute (ANSI). Establishes a basic vocabulary for the theory and application of terminology work. It was reaffirmed in 2010 without revision as ANSI/NISO Z39.19-2005 (R2010), and is known by a variety of designations similar to that one. The full title is *Guidelines for the Construction, Format, and Management of Monolingual Controlled Vocabularies*. The 2010 version is referred to in this book as Z39.19-2010R.

Ant colony optimization (ACO)

> An algorithmic approach to task optimization based on the behavior of ants. The probability that an ant will choose a particular path is proportional to the number of times that other ants have already chosen that path, creating a positive feedback loop. ACO algorithms are being developed and researched for a wide variety of task optimization problems, including data classification.

API (Application programming interface)

> Programming code that a computer system provides for supporting requests made of that system by a computer program. Often used to refer to the software that implements an API.

Associative relationship

> As defined in ANSI/NISO Z39.19-2010R, "*A relationship between or among terms in a controlled vocabulary that leads from one term to other terms that are related to or associated with it.*" A pair of terms that have an associative relationship is known as related terms; this relationship is often indicated by the acronym "RT."

Author submission system, Submission management system

> An online platform on which authors can submit articles and associated information directly to a publisher (usually of an online article database). Often, this same platform can also be used by the editorial staff to manage peer review, internal and author review of the draft and proposed changes, and other workflow aspects of the publication process.

Authority file, Authority list

> As defined in ANSI/NISO Z39.19-2010R, "*A set of established headings and the cross-references to be made to and from each heading, often citing the authority for the preferred form or variants. Types of authority files include name authority files and subject authority files.*"

Auto-categorization, Auto-Indexing

> Computer-automated subject indexing.

Auto-completion

> In search interfaces, a feature that produces a display of possible search words or phrases, sometimes based on an associated taxonomy or thesaurus, when a user starts typing a search string. In Google and similar search platforms, the completion is based on previous queries.

Bayes' Theorem

> A major statistical principle, involving the calculation of probability based on prior statistical evidence.

Bayesian search

> In information retrieval, the use of probability calculation methods based on Bayes' theorem to determine the likelihood of potential information resources being relevant to specific searches.

Binomial nomenclature (Binominal nomenclature, Binary nomenclature)

The standard system used by biologists for designating biological organisms with two-word Latin or pseudo-Latin names. The first word indicates the genus to which an organism is assumed to belong, and the second word indicates the appropriate species name within that genus.

Boolean algebra, Boolean logic

A form of algebra in which logical expressions contain one or more Boolean operators (AND, OR, NOT) to define sets.

Boolean search

A type of information search that uses the operators of Boolean logic (AND, OR, NOT), in combination with two or more search strings, to filter search results.

Bottom-up approach (in controlled vocabulary construction)

As explained in ANSI/NISO Z39.19-2010R, "*the necessary hierarchical structures and relationships are created as the work proceeds, but starting from the terms having the narrowest scope and moving to the more generic ones.*"

British Standards Institution, BSI (aka BSI Group)

The organization officially recognized by the government of the United Kingdom as the U.K.'s National Standards Body. BSI is the U.K. member of the international standards organizations, ISO and IEC.

Broader term

As defined in ANSI/NISO Z39.19-2010R, "*A term to which another term or multiple terms are subordinate in a hierarchy. In thesauri, the relationship indicator for this type of term is BT.*"

Browsing

As defined in ANSI/NISO Z39.19-2010R, "*The process of visually scanning through organized collections of representations of content objects, controlled vocabulary terms, hierarchies, taxonomies, thesauri, etc.*"

Candidate term

As defined in ANSI/NISO Z39.19-2010R, "*A term under consideration for admission into a controlled vocabulary because of its potential usefulness.*"

Classification scheme

As defined in ANSI/NISO Z39.19-2010R, "*A method of organization according to a set of pre-established principles, usually characterized by a notation system and a hierarchical structure of relationships among the entities.*"

Collabulary

As defined by Jonathon Keats, "*A collaborative vocabulary for tagging Web content. Like the folksonomies used on social bookmarking sites like del.icio.us [now Delicious], collabularies are generated by a community. But unlike folksonomies, they're automatically vetted for consistency, extracting the wisdom of crowds from the cacophony.*" (Jonathon Keats, "Jargon Watch," *Wired*, January 1, 2007)

Colon classification

A library classification system developed by S.R. Ranganathan. It is reputed to be the first faceted classification system.

Compound term

As defined in ANSI/NISO Z39.19-2010R, "*A term consisting of more than one word that represents a single concept.*"

Controlled vocabulary

As defined in ANSI/NISO Z39.19-2010R:

"*A list of terms that have been enumerated explicitly. This list is controlled by and is available from a controlled vocabulary registration authority. All terms in a controlled vocabulary must have an un-ambiguous, non-redundant definition.* **NOTE**: *This is a design goal that may not be true in practice; it depends on how strict the controlled vocabulary registration authority is regarding registration of terms into a controlled vocabulary.*

"*At a minimum, the following two rules must be enforced:*

"*1. If the same term is commonly used to mean different concepts, then its name is explicitly qualified to resolve this ambiguity.* **NOTE**: *This rule does not apply to synonym rings.*

"*2. If multiple terms are used to mean the same thing, one of the terms is identified as the preferred term in the controlled vocabulary and the other terms are listed as synonyms or aliases.*"

"Registration authority" refers to any taxonomy editor or taxonomy team that has some sort of authorization for control of the vocabulary, or the organization granting them the authority, will serve the purpose.

COSATI

The Federal Council on Science and Technology's Committee on Scientific and Technical Information. It was operational from the early 1960s to the early 1970s.

Cutter Expansive Classification (often referred to as **Cutter classification)**

A library classification system developed by Charles Ammi Cutter in the 1880s. It serves as the basis for the Library of Congress Classification.

Data visualization

The use of a graphical visual representation to convey or interpret data.

DCMI

See Dublin Core Metadata Initiative.

Descriptor

See Preferred term.

Dewey Decimal Classification (commonly known as the **Dewey Decimal System)**

A library classification system developed by Melvil Dewey in the 1870s and 1880s. It formed the basis of the Universal Decimal Classification.

Dublin Core, Dublin Core Metadata Element Set

As described by the Dublin Core Metadata Initiative at http://dublincore.org/documents/dces/, "*The Dublin Core Metadata Element Set is a vocabulary of fifteen properties for use in resource description. The name 'Dublin' is due to its origin at a 1995 invitational workshop in Dublin, Ohio; 'core' because its elements are broad and generic, usable for describing a wide range of resources.*" This core metadata element set is usually referred to as "Dublin Core."

Dublin Core Metadata Initiative (DCMI)

According to DCMI's website (http://dublincore.org/), "*The Dublin Core Metadata Initiative, or 'DCMI,' is an open organization supporting innovation in metadata design and best practices across the metadata ecology. DCMI's activities include work on architecture and modeling, discussions and collaborative work in DCMI Communities and DCMI Task Groups, global conferences, meetings and workshops, and educational efforts to promote widespread acceptance of metadata standards and best practices.*" DCMI is the main promulgator of the Dublin Core metadata standards.

Editorial note

A note connected with a controlled vocabulary term (usually in a designated field in the term record), for the purpose of communicating information having to do with in-house editorial and vocabulary development matters. Editorial notes are generally not exposed to Internet display.

Enterprise software

Software designed for use by several people simultaneously within an organization.

Entry term, Non-preferred term

A synonym or quasi-synonym for a preferred term. Non-preferred terms are not used for indexing, but can direct a manual indexer or an automated indexing system to use the corresponding preferred terms. "Entry terms" (but not "non-preferred terms") may also be considered to include indexing terms.

Epistemology, Theory of knowledge

The philosophical field covering the study of the nature of knowledge.

Equivalence relationship

As defined in ANSI/NISO Z39.19-2010R, "*A relationship between or among terms in a controlled vocabulary that leads to one or more terms that are to be used instead of the term from which the cross-reference is made.*"

Faceted classification, Faceted taxonomy

A method of taxonomic classification in which terms or subjects are placed in a variety of mutually exclusive categories (such as color or location), in order to reflect various aspects or dimensions of each subject.

Faceted search, Fielded search

Search of information organized or indexed according to a faceted classification system, allowing multiple filters for narrowing of the search according to variety of dimensions or aspects. Often used in e-commerce.

Hierarchical relationship

As defined in ANSI/NISO Z39.19-2010R, "*A relationship between or among terms in a controlled vocabulary that depicts broader (generic) to narrower (specific) or whole–part relationships; begins with the words broader term (BT), or narrower term (NT).*"

Hierarchy

As defined in ANSI/NISO Z39.19-2010R, "*Broader (generic) to narrower (specific) or whole–part relationships, which are generally indicated in a controlled vocabulary through codes or indentation.*"

Homograph

As defined in ANSI/NISO Z39.19-2010R: "*One of two or more words that have the same spelling, but different meanings and origins. In controlled vocabularies, homographs are generally distinguished by qualifiers.*" I discourage the use of qualifiers, and encourage the use of other means whenever possible to differentiate homograms (homographs).

Indexing

As defined in ANSI/NISO Z39.19-2010R, "*A method by which terms or subject headings from a controlled vocabulary are selected by a human or computer to represent the concepts in or attributes of a content object. The terms may or may not occur in the content object.*" This kind of indexing should not be confused with indexing processes for creating a book index or a data index.

Indexing term

As defined in ANSI/NISO Z39.19-2010R, "*The representation of a concept in an indexing language, generally in the form of a noun or noun phrase. Terms, subject headings, and heading-subheading combinations are examples of indexing terms. Also called descriptor.*"

Keyword

As defined in ANSI/NISO Z39.19-2010R, "*A word occurring in the natural language of a document that is considered significant for indexing and retrieval.*" Keywords can be assigned to a work by its author(s), or can be words used in search queries.

LCSH

See *Library of Congress Subject Headings*.

Library of Congress Classification

The system of library classification developed and maintained by the Library of Congress. It is used by many university and research libraries, as well as by the Library of Congress, for classifying library holdings.

Library of Congress Subject Headings (LCSH)

A thesaurus of subject headings maintained and used by the Library of Congress for subject metadata in library catalog records.

Linked data

Structured data that is connected with other data resources, based on some relationships considered to be useful, with each piece of data identified by an http URI.

Literary warrant (See also User warrant, Organizational warrant)

As defined in ANSI/NISO Z39.19-2010R, "*Justification for the representation of a concept in an indexing language or for the selection of a preferred term because of its frequent occurrence in the literature.*"

MARC (Machine-Readable Cataloging)

A set of digital formats for the bibliographic description of library holdings, developed by the Library of Congress and now an international standard.

Machine-assisted indexing

Indexing using software that suggests indexing terms from one or more controlled vocabularies, but that allows a human indexer to make the final determination as to which terms will be used for indexing of each resource.

MeSH (Medical Subject Headings)

A thesaurus of subject headings developed and maintained by the U.S. National Library of Medicine (NLM), and used by NLM for cataloging MEDLINE and PubMed articles.

Metadata

There are many kinds of metadata. Metadata is data about data—it provides the overview of an item. This book mostly refers to subject metadata from a thesaurus but descriptive metadata is the most common usage. Descriptive metadata is used to provide descriptive information about information resources. In bibliographic records and similar metadata records, the terms for the subject metadata record fields are typically obtained from a taxonomy, thesaurus, or similar classification scheme. In addition to subject and descriptive metadata, records can contain structural metadata and administrative metadata.

Narrower term

As defined in ANSI/NISO Z39.19-2010R, "*A term that is subordinate to another term or to multiple terms in a hierarchy. In thesauri, the relationship indicator for this type of term is NT.*"

National Information Standards Organization (NISO)

As NISO describes itself at http://www.niso.org/about/, "*NISO, the National Information Standards Organization, a non-profit association accredited by the American National Standards Institute (ANSI), identifies, develops, maintains, and publishes technical standards to manage information in our changing and ever-more digital environment. NISO standards apply both traditional and new technologies to the full range of information-related needs, including retrieval, re-purposing, storage, metadata, and preservation.*"

Natural language

As defined in ANSI/NISO Z39.19-2010R, "*A language used by human beings for verbal communication. Words extracted from natural language texts for indexing purposes without vocabulary control are often called keywords.*"

Natural language processing (NLP)

Computer processing of text presented in natural language.

Navigation (See also **Browsing)**

As defined in ANSI/NISO Z39.19-2010R, "*The process of moving through a controlled vocabulary or an information space via some pre-established links or relationships. For example, navigation in a controlled vocabulary could mean moving from a broader term to one or more narrower terms using the predefined relationships.*"

NISO, National Information Standards Organization

As NISO describes itself at http://www.niso.org/about/, "*NISO, the National Information Standards Organization, a non-profit association accredited by the American National Standards Institute (ANSI), identifies, develops, maintains, and publishes technical standards to manage information in our changing and ever-more digital environment. NISO standards apply both traditional and new technologies to the full range of information-related needs, including retrieval, re-purposing, storage, metadata, and preservation.*"

NLP

See *Natural language processing.*

Node label

As defined in ANSI/NISO Z39.19-2010R, "*A 'dummy' term, often a phrase, that is not assigned to documents when indexing, but which is inserted into the hierarchical section of some controlled vocabularies to indicate the logical basis on which a class has been divided. Node labels may also be used to group categories of related terms in the alphabetic section of a controlled vocabulary."*

Non-preferred term, Entry term

A synonym or quasi-synonym for a preferred term. Non-preferred terms are not used for indexing, but can direct a manual indexer or an automated indexing system to use the corresponding preferred terms. "Entry terms" (but not "non-preferred terms") may also be considered to include indexing terms.

ONIX (Online Information eXchange)

As described by EDitEUR, one of several organizations involved in the development of ONIX, *"an XML-based family of international standards intended to support computer-to-computer communication between parties involved in creating, distributing, licensing or otherwise making available intellectual property in published form, whether physical or digital."*

Ontology

As explained by the World Wide Web Consortium (W3C) at http://www.w3.org/standards/semanticweb/ontology, *"There is no clear division between what is referred to as 'vocabularies' and 'ontologies.' The trend is to use the word 'ontology' for more complex, and possibly quite formal collection of terms, whereas 'vocabulary' is used when such strict formalism is not necessarily used or only in a very loose sense."*

Organizational warrant (See also **User warrant, Literary warrant)**

As defined in ANSI/NISO Z39.19-2010R, *"Justification for the representation of a concept in an indexing language or for the selection of a preferred term due to characteristics and context of the organization."*

OWL (Web Ontology Language)

An XML-based format designed by the World Wide Web Consortium (W3C) for use in ontologies. As described by W3C at http://www.w3.org/standards/techs/owl#w3c_all, *"The OWL Web Ontology Language is designed for use by applications that need to process the content of information instead of just presenting information to humans. OWL facilitates greater machine interpretability of Web content than that supported by XML, RDF, and RDF Schema (RDF-S) by providing additional vocabulary along with a formal semantics. OWL has three increasingly-expressive sublanguages: OWL Lite, OWL DL, and OWL Full."*

Permuted display

As defined in Z39.19, *"A type of index where individual words of a term are rotated to bring each word of the term into alphabetical order in the term list."*

Polyhierarchy

The property of a taxonomy or thesaurus whereby a term can exist in more than one place in the overall hierarchical structure, having multiple broader terms.

Post-coordination

As defined in ANSI/NISO Z39.19-2010R, "*The combining of terms at the searching stage rather than at the subject heading list construction stage or indexing stage.*"

Pre-coordination

As defined in ANSI/NISO Z39.19-2010R, "*The formulation of a multiword heading or the linking of a heading and subheadings to create a formally controlled, multi-element expression of a concept or object.*"

Precision (in search results)

As defined in ANSI/NISO Z39.19-2010R, "*A measure of a search system's ability to retrieve only relevant content objects. Usually expressed as a percentage calculated by dividing the number of retrieved relevant content objects by the total number of content objects retrieved.*"

Preferred term

As defined in ANSI/NISO Z39.19-2010R, "*One of two or more synonyms or lexical variants selected as a term for inclusion in a controlled vocabulary.*"

Provisional term

See *Candidate term.*

RDA (Resource Description and Access)

A set of guidelines published jointly in 2010 by the American Library Association, the Canadian Library Association, and the U.K.'s Chartered Institute of Library and Information Professionals, and intended to replace the *Anglo-American Cataloguing Rules*, 2nd Edition (AACR2).

RDF (Resource Description Framework)

As described by the World Wide Web Consortium (W3C) at http://www.w3.org/RDF/, "*RDF is a standard model for data interchange on the Web. RDF has features that facilitate data merging even if the underlying schemas differ, and it specifically supports the evolution of schemas over time without requiring all the data consumers to be changed. RDF extends the linking structure of the Web to use URIs to name the relationship between things as well as the two ends of the link (this is usually referred to as a 'triple'). Using this simple model, it allows structured and semi-structured data to be mixed, exposed, and shared across different applications.*"

Recall (in search results)

As defined in ANSI/NISO Z39.19, "*A measure of a search system's ability to retrieve all relevant content objects. Usually expressed as a percentage calculated by dividing the number of retrieved relevant content objects by the number of all relevant content objects in a collection.*"

Reciprocity (of term relationships)

As explained in ANSI/NISO Z39.19, "*Semantic relationships in controlled vocabularies must be reciprocal, that is each relationship from one term to another must also be represented by a recip-*

rocal relationship in the other direction. Reciprocal relationships may be symmetric, e.g. RT / RT, or asymmetric e.g., BT/NT."

Related term

As defined in ANSI/NISO Z39.19, *"A term that is associatively but not hierarchically linked to another term in a controlled vocabulary."* It is intended to expand the searcher's awareness of the vocabulary, suggesting other concepts that may be of interest.

Resource Description and Access

See RDA.

Scope note

As defined in ANSI/NISO Z39.19-2010R, *"A note following a term explaining its coverage, specialized usage, or rules for assigning it."*

Semantic Web

As described by the World Wide Web Consortium (W3C) at http://www.w3.org/2001/sw/, *"The Semantic Web is about two things. It is about common formats for integration and combination of data drawn from diverse sources, where on the original Web mainly concentrated on the interchange of documents. It is also about language for recording how the data relates to real world objects. That allows a person, or a machine, to start off in one database, and then move through an unending set of databases which are connected not by wires but by being about the same thing."*

SKOS (Simple Knowledge Organization System)

According to the World Wide Web Consortium (W3C) at http://www.w3.org/TR/skos-reference/, *"a common data model for sharing and linking knowledge organization systems via the Web. Many knowledge organization systems, such as thesauri, taxonomies, classification schemes and subject heading systems, share a similar structure, and are used in similar applications. SKOS captures much of this similarity and makes it explicit, to enable data and technology sharing across diverse applications. The SKOS data model provides a standard, low-cost migration path for porting existing knowledge organization systems to the Semantic Web. SKOS also provides a lightweight, intuitive language for developing and sharing new knowledge organization systems. It may be used on its own, or in combination with formal knowledge representation languages such as the Web Ontology language (OWL)."*

Structured data

Data in which the text of each information resource is partitioned into fields, often delimited by XML "tags" or field labels indicating the kind of metadata element contained within each field.

Subject heading

As explained in ANSI/NISO Z39.19-2010R: *"A word or phrase, or any combination of words, phrases, and modifiers used to describe the topic of a content object. Precoordination of terms for multiple and related concepts is a characteristic of subject headings that distinguishes them from controlled vocabulary terms.*"

Subject matter expert (SME)

In taxonomy and thesaurus development, a person who has deep knowledge of a subject area represented in the vocabulary, and who provides advice and feedback regarding such matters as term wording, hierarchical structure, appropriate non-preferred terms, and terms or concepts to consider adding.

Synonym ring

As defined in ANSI/NISO Z39.19-2010R, "*A group of terms that are considered equivalent for the purposes of retrieval.*" Terms in a synonym ring are not distinguished as preferred or non-preferred.

Taxonomy

As defined in ANSI/NISO Z39.19-2010R, "*A collection of controlled vocabulary terms organized into a hierarchical structure. Each term in a taxonomy is in one or more parent/child (broader/narrower) relationships to other terms in the taxonomy.*"

Term

As defined in ANSI/NISO Z39.19-2010R, "*One or more words designating a concept.*"

Terminology registry

A descriptive catalog of terminologies, usually containing taxonomies and thesauri, as well as other kinds of controlled vocabularies.

Theory of knowledge

See Epistemology.

Thesaurus (plural Thesauri or Thesauruses)

As defined in ANSI/NISO Z39.19-2010R, "*A controlled vocabulary arranged in a known order and structured so that the various relationships among terms are displayed clearly and identified by standardized relationship indicators.*"

Top-down approach (in controlled vocabulary construction)

As explained in ANSI/NISO Z39.19-2010R, "*The broadest terms are identified first and then narrower terms are selected to reach the desired level of specificity. The necessary hierarchical structures and relationships are created as the work proceeds.*"

Training set

A set of documents used in developing the indexing capabilities of a statistics-based indexing system.

Truncation

Shortening of a word or phrase, sometimes replacing the omitted portion with a wildcard character that can represent any and all characters. This technique is used to give more comprehensive results when creating search strings or indexing rules.

Turney's algorithm

A semantic approach to sentiment analysis. A *"simple unsupervised learning algorithm for classifying reviews as recommended (thumbs up) or not recommended (thumbs down). The classification of a review is predicted by the average semantic orientation of the phrases in the review that contain adjectives or adverbs. A phrase has a positive semantic orientation when it has good associations (e.g., 'subtle nuances') and a negative semantic orientation when it has bad associations (e.g., 'very cavalier')"* (In Peter D. Turney, "Thumbs Up or Thumbs Down? Semantic Orientation Applied to Unsupervised Classification of Reviews," *Proceedings of the 40th Annual Meeting of the Association for Computational Linguistics*, Philadelphia, July 2002: 417–424).

UID

Unique identifier. An identification number or alphanumeric code often used with taxonomy and thesaurus terms, term records, and concept records.

Unicode

As described by Unicode, Inc., at http://www.unicode.org/standard/standard.html, *"The Unicode Standard is a character coding system designed to support the worldwide interchange, processing, and display of the written texts of the diverse languages and technical disciplines of the modern world. In addition, it supports classical and historical texts of many written languages."*

Universal Decimal Classification (UDC)

As described by the UDC Consortium at www.udcc.org, *"UDC is one of the most widely used classification schemes for all fields of knowledge. It is used in libraries, bibliographic, documentation and information services in over 130 countries around the world and is published in over 40 languages."*

Unstructured text

See *Structured text*. Unstructured text lacks such metadata labeling.

User warrant

As defined in ANSI/NISO Z39.19-2010R, *"Justification for the representation of a concept in an indexing language or for the selection of a preferred term because of frequent requests for information on the concept or free-text searches on the term by users of an information storage and retrieval system."*

Vocabulary control

As defined in ANSI/NISO Z39.19-2010R: *"The process of organizing a list of terms (a) to indicate which of two or more synonymous terms is authorized for use; (b) to distinguish between homographs; and (c) to indicate hierarchical and associative relationships among terms in the context of a controlled vocabulary or subject heading list.*"

W3C, World Wide Web Consortium

As described by W3C at http://www.w3.org/Consortium/, "*The World Wide Web Consortium (W3C) is an international community where Member organizations, a full-time staff, and the public work together to develop Web standards. Led by Web inventor Tim Berners-Lee and CEO Jeffrey Jaffe, W3C's mission is to lead the Web to its full potential.*"

Web Ontology Language (OWL)

An XML-based format designed by the World Wide Web Consortium (W3C) for use in ontologies. As described by W3C at http://www.w3.org/standards/techs/owl#w3c_all, "*The OWL Web Ontology Language is designed for use by applications that need to process the content of information instead of just presenting information to humans. OWL facilitates greater machine interpretability of Web content than that supported by XML, RDF, and RDF Schema (RDF-S) by providing additional vocabulary along with a formal semantics. OWL has three increasingly-expressive sublanguages: OWL Lite, OWL DL, and OWL Full.*"

Z39.19 (ANSI/NISO Z39.19)

Taxonomy and thesaurus standard developed by the National Information Standards Organization (NISO), and approved July 25, 2005, by the American National Standards Institute (ANSI). Establishes a basic vocabulary for the theory and application of terminology work. It was reaffirmed in 2010 without revision as ANSI/NISO Z39.19-2005 (R2010), and is known by a variety of designations similar to that one. The full title is *Guidelines for the Construction, Format, and Management of Monolingual Controlled Vocabularies.* The 2010 version is referred to in this book as Z39.19-2010R. It does not embrace the vocabulary dealing with computer applications in terminology work which was covered by withdrawn standard ISO 1087-2.

End Notes

1   Lars Marius Garshol, "Metadata? Thesauri? Taxonomies? Topic Maps! Making Sense of it All." *Journal of Information Science* 30., no. 4 (August 2004), 379.

2   http://en.wikipedia.org/wiki/Aboutness.

3   "A mashup, in web development, is a webpage, or web application, that uses content from more than one source to create a single new service displayed in a single graphical interface. For example, you could combine the addresses and photographs of your library branches with a Google map to create a map mashup. The term implies easy, fast integration, frequently using open application programming interfaces (open APIs) and data sources to produce enriched results that were not necessarily the original reason for producing the raw source data. . . . In recent English parlance it can refer to music, where people seamlessly combine audio from one song with the vocal track from another—thereby mashing them together to create something new."

"The main characteristics of a mashup are combination, visualization, and aggregation. It is important to make existing data more useful, for personal and professional use. To be able to permanently access the data of other services, mashups are generally client applications or hosted online." http://en.wikipedia.org/wiki/Mashup_(web_application_hybrid).

4   Jean Aitchison, Alan Gilchrist, and David Bawden in the 4th edition of *Thesaurus Construction and Use: a Practical Manual*, (ASLIB IMI, 2000), 1.

5   http://en.wikipedia.org/wiki/Richard_Saul_Wurman.

6   National Information Standards Organization (NISO), ANSI/NISO Z39.19, *Guidelines for the Construction, Format, and Management of Monolingual Controlled Vocabularies*, (NISO Press, 2005 [reaffirmed 2010]), 12.

7   National Information Standards Organization, ANSI/NISO Z39.19, *Guidelines for the Construction, Format, and Management of Monolingual Controlled Vocabularies*, (NISO Press, 2005 [reaffirmed 2010]), 6.

8   ANSI/NISO Z39.19, 12.

9   http://en.wikipedia.org/wiki/Folksonomy.

10   http://id.loc.gov/authorities/subjects.html.

11   http://www.ebscohost.com/academic/sears-list-of-subject-headings.

12   http://www.oclc.org/dewey/resources/summaries.en.html.

13   "Outline of Knowledge," *Wikipedia*, http://en.wikipedia.org/wiki/Outline_of_knowledge as accessed on November 5, 2013.

14   "ORCID provides a persistent digital identifier that distinguishes you from every other researcher and, through integration in key research workflows such as manuscript and grant submission, supports automated linkages between you and your professional activities ensuring that your work is recognized." http://orcid.org/.

15   "VIVO enables the discovery of researchers across institutions. Participants in the network include institutions with local installations of VIVO or those with research discovery and profiling applications that can provide semantic web-compliant data. The information accessible through VIVO's search and browse capability will reside and be controlled locally, within institutional VIVOs or other semantic web-compliant applications." http://vivoweb.org/about.

16   "The VIAF™ (Virtual International Authority File) combines multiple name authority files into a single OCLC-hosted name authority service. The goal of the service is to lower the cost and increase the utility of library authority files by matching and linking widely-used authority files and making that information available on the Web." http://viaf.org/.

17   "The term knowledge organization systems is intended to encompass all types of schemes for organizing information and promoting knowledge management. Knowledge organization systems include classification schemes that organize materials at a general level (such as books on a shelf), subject headings that provide more detailed access, and authority files that control variant versions of key information (such as geographic names and personal names). They also include less-traditional schemes, such as semantic networks and ontologies." http://www.clir.org/pubs/reports/pub91/1knowledge.html.

18   "RDF is a standard model for data interchange on the Web. RDF has features that facilitate data merging even if the underlying schemas differ, and it specifically supports the evolution of schemas over time without requiring all the data consumers to be changed." http://www.w3.org/RDF/.

19   "The OWL Web Ontology Language is designed for use by applications that need to process the content of information instead of just presenting information to humans. OWL facilitates greater machine interpretability of Web content than that supported by XML, RDF, and RDF Schema (RDF-S) by providing additional expressive power along with a formal semantics." http://www.w3.org/2007/OWL/wiki/OWL_Working_Group.

20   "SKOS is an area of work developing specifications and standards to support the use of knowledge organization systems (KOS) such as thesauri, classification schemes, subject heading systems and taxonomies within the framework of the Semantic Web." http://www.w3.org/2004/02/skos/intro.

21   Retrieved at http://www.w3.org/standards/semanticweb/ontology on July 30, 2013.

22   Heather Hedden, *The Accidental Taxonomist*, 14.

23   http://protege.stanford.edu/.

24   NISO 2004.

25   Dublin Core Metadata Initiative, 2007.

26   http://www.loc.gov/marc/umb/.

27   http://www.aacr2.org/.

28   http://www.rdatoolkit.org/examples/MARC.

29   "Interoperability of data in e-commerce systems" developed in 2000 by the European community building on the BISAC (Book Industry Subject and Category) Subject Headings built by the Book Industry Study group, BISG, and Edituer.

30   http://www.doi.org/topics/indecs/indecs_framework_2000.pdf.

31   http://www.w3.org/RDF/.

32   http://www.tei-c.org/index.xml.

33   http://www.ukoln.ac.uk/metadata/roads/cataloguing/.

34   http://www.rdatoolkit.org/about.

35   Founded in 1967 as the **Ohio College Library Center**, now the **Online Computer Library Center, Inc.** (OCLC).

36   http://www.niso.org/apps/group_public/project/details.php?project_id=57.

37   ISO 15836:2009 The Dublin Core metadata element set.

38   http://www.ietf.org/.

39   http://www.dialog.com/about/.

40   http://en.wikipedia.org/wiki/BRS/Search, currently owned by http://www.opentext.com/.

41   The combination of System Development Corporation (SDC) and ORBIT Search Service Databases, both now defunct.

42   http://www.loc.gov/standards/iso639-2/php/code_list.php.

43   http://www.iana.org/assignments/media-types.

44   http://www.w3.org/People/Berners-Lee/.

45   http://home.web.cern.ch/.

46   Brewster Kahle, Harry Morris, Jonathan Goldman, Thomas Erickson, and John Curran, "Interfaces for distributed systems of information servers." *Journal of the American Society for Information Science* 44, no. 8 (1993): 453–467. DOI: DOI: 10.1002/(SICI)1097-4571(199309)44:8<453::AID-ASI4>3.0.CO;2-E.

47   An SGML declaration defines the coding scheme used in its preparation. http://www.is-thought.co.uk/book/sgml-4.htm#Purpose.

48   "A document type definition (DTD) is a set of *markup declarations* that define a *document type* for an SGML-family markup language (SGML, XML, HTML). A DTD uses a terse formal syntax that declares precisely which elements and references may appear where in the document of the particular type, and what the elements' contents and attributes are. A DTD can also declare entities that may be used in the *instance* document." http://en.wikipedia.org/wiki/Document_type_definition.

49   http://www.loc.gov/ead/ead2002a.html.

50   http://www.tei-c.org/Vault/P4/Lite/DTD/teixlite.dtd.

51   http://jats.nlm.nih.gov/.

52   The SGML declaration for HTML 4.0, from http://www.w3.org/TR/WD-html40-970917/sgml/sgmldecl.html.

53   A schema is a model for describing the structure of information. http://www.webopedia.com/TERM/X/XSD.html.

54   http://wordnet.princeton.edu/.

55   http://en.wikipedia.org/wiki/Recombination.

56   In "Taxonomy Disaster Stories" at "Learning for a Living: Jean Graef's Point of View," April 15, 2013. Accessed at http://montagueinstitute.wordpress.com/2013/04/15/taxonomy-disaster-stories/ on July 17, 2013.

57   http://www.nlm.nih.gov/mesh/.

58   http://www.nlm.nih.gov/research/umls/knowledge_sources/metathesaurus/.

59   Carl Lagoze, "Accommodating Simplicity and Complexity in Metadata: Lessons from the Dublin Core Experience." Presented at Seminar on Metadata, organized by Archiefschool, Netherlands Institute for Archival Education and Research, June 8, 2000. Ac-

cessed at https://ecommons.library.cornell.edu/bitstream/1813/5792/1/2000-1801.pdf on May 30, 2013. DOI: 10.1.1.89.2375.

60 Geoffrey Bowker and Susan Leigh Star. *Sorting Things Out: Classification and its Consequences*. Cambridge: MIT Press, 1999.

61 ANSI/NISO Z39.19-2010R, p. 16.

62 ANSI/NISO Z39.19-2010R, p. 16.

63 ANSI/NISO Z39.19-2010R, p. 16.

64 Clay Shirky, "*Ontology is Overrated: Categories, Links, and Tags.*" Accessed at http://www.shirky.com/writings/ontology_overrated.html on October 21, 2013.

65 COSATI is now part of CENDI, http://www.cendi.gov/about/history.html.

66 http://www.aip.org/pacs/.

67 http://www.opticsinfobase.org/submit/ocis/OCIS_2007.pdf.

68 From "Capitalization in Taxonomies," *The Accidental Taxonomist* (blog) http://accidental-taxonomist.blogspot.com/search/label/Editorial%20style.

69 "Recombination," *Wikipedia*, http://en.wikipedia.org/wiki/Recombination, accessed on October 21, 2013.

70 *Thesauri and Interoperability with other Vocabularies, Part 1: Thesauri for Information Retrieval.*

71 "Node labels, or "dummy" terms, often expressed as phrases, are inserted into the hierarchical section of each thesaurus to indicate the logical basis on which a class has been divided. Node labels may also be used to group categories of related terms in the alphabetic section of a thesaurus." http://www.rbms.info/rbms_manual/thesaurus_construction.shtml.

72 ANSI/NISO Z39.19-2010R, p. 91.

73 "How Do I Build a Thesaurus?" http://www.asindexing.org/i4a/pages/index.cfm?pageid=3623.

74 F. Wilfrid Lancaster, *Thesaurus Construction and Use: A Condensed Course*, General Information Program and UNISIST, United Nations Educational, Scientific and Cultural Organization, 1985, p. 10.

75 Leonard Will, correspondence in the JISCMail—TAXONOMY Archives.

76 http://en.wikipedia.org/wiki/Three-click_rule.

77 ANSI/NISO Z39.19, p. 49.

78	ANSI/NISO Z39.19-2010R, pp. 49–50.
79	http://en.wikipedia.org/wiki/Jorn_Barger.
80	http://en.wikipedia.org/wiki/Blog.
81	http://www.niso.org/standards/resources/Z39-19.html.
82	http://www.niso.org/schemas/iso25964/.
83	http://www.w3.org/TR/owl-features/.
84	http://www.w3.org/standards/techs/skos#w3c_all.
85	http://www.iso.org/iso/home/store/catalogue_tc/catalogue_detail.htm?csnumber=38109.
86	http://www.iso.org/iso/home/store/catalogue_tc/catalogue_detail.htm?csnumber=40130.
87	http://www.iso.org/iso/home/store/catalogue_tc/catalogue_detail.htm?csnumber=20057.
88	http://www.iso.org/iso/home/store/catalogue_tc/catalogue_detail.htm?csnumber=36143.
89	http://www.iso.org/iso/home/store/catalogue_tc/catalogue_detail.htm?csnumber=42040.
90	http://www.iso.org/iso/home/store/catalogue_tc/catalogue_detail.htm?csnumber=53787.
91	http://www.iso.org/iso/home.html.
92	According to ISO, "ISO" is not an abbreviation. It is a word, derived from the Greek isos, meaning "equal", which is the root for the prefix "iso-" that occurs in a host of terms, such as "isometric" (of equal measure or dimensions) and "isonomy" (equality of laws, or of people before the law). The name ISO is used around the world to denote the organization, thus avoiding the assortment of abbreviations that would result from the translation of "International Organization for Standardization" into the different national languages of members. Whatever the country, the short form of the organization's name is always ISO. From http://searchdatacenter.techtarget.com/definition/ISO.
93	http://www.ansi.org/.
94	http://www.niso.org/home/.
95	http://www.iso.org/iso/home/standards_development.htm.
96	http://www.iso.org/iso/home/standards_development/list_of_iso_technical_committees/iso_technical_committee.htm?commid=48750.
97	http://www.iso.org/iso/home/standards_development/list_of_iso_technical_committees/iso_technical_committee.htm?commid=48104.

98   The World Wide Web Consortium (W3C) is an international community where Member organizations, a full-time staff, and the public work together to develop Web standards. From www.w3.org.

99   We owe the email and internet protocols to the W3C. Standards such as Web Ontology Language (OWL) and SKOS (Simple Knowledge Organization System) also come from the W3C.

100   http://www.webopedia.com/TERM/T/TCP_IP.html.

101   The International Federation of Library Associations and Institutions (IFLA) is the leading international body representing the interests of library and information services and their users. It is the global voice of the library and information profession. http://www.loc.gov/standards/.

102   http://www.ifla.org/.

103   http://www.ifla.org/publications/functional-requirements-for-bibliographic-records.

104   http://www.beuth.de/en/standard/nf-z47-100/12316890.

105   http://www.beuth.de/en/standard/oenorm-din-1463-1/7118470.

106   http://comminfo.rutgers.edu/~jda/anderson.html.

107   http://www.niso.org/publications/tr/tr02.pdf.

108   http://www.cendi.gov/about/history.html.

109   http://www.nixonlibrary.gov/forresearchers/find/textual/central/subject/FG119.php.

110   http://www.dtic.mil/dtic/tr/fulltext/u2/661001.pdf.

111   http://en.wikipedia.org/wiki/Alvin_M._Weinberg.

112   http://www.beuth.de/en/standard/nf-z47-100/12316890.

113   http://www.beuth.de/en/standard/oenorm-din-1463-1/7118470.

114   http://www.asis.org/Bulletin/Oct-08/OctNov08_DextreClark.pdf, http://metadaten-twr.org/tag/iso-25964/, http://www.niso.org/workrooms/iso25964, http://www.niso.org/schemas/iso25964/.

115   ISO 25964-1 "Information and documentation—Thesauri and interoperability with other vocabularies—Part 1: Thesauri for information retrieval," http://www.niso.org/schemas/iso25964/#part1.

116   ISO 25964-2 "Information and documentation—Thesauri and interoperability with other vocabularies—Part 2: Interoperability," http://www.niso.org/schemas/iso25964/#part2.

117   www.iso.org.

118 www.iso.org.

Author Biography

Marjorie M.K. Hlava and her team have worked with or built over 600 controlled vocabularies. Their experience is shared with you in this book. Margie is well known internationally for her work in the implementation of information science principles and the ever-evolving technology that supports them. She and the team at Access Innovations have provided the "back room" operations for many information-related organizations over the last 40 years. Margie is very active in the main organizations concerned with those areas. She has served as president of NFAIS (the National Federation of Advanced Information Services); that organization awarded her the Anne Marie Cunningham Memorial Award for Exemplary Volunteer Service to the Federation in 2012, as well as the Miles Conrad lectureship in 2014. She has also served as president of the American Society for Information Science and Technology (ASIS&T), which has awarded her the prestigious Watson Davis Award. She has served two terms on the Board of Directors of the Special Libraries Association (SLA); SLA has honored her with their President's Award for her work in standards and has made her a Fellow of the SLA for her many other services within the organization. More recently, she served as the founding chair of SLA's Taxonomy Division.

For five years, Margie was on the Board of the National Information Standards Organization (NISO), and she continues to serve on the Content and Collaboration Standards Topic Committee for NISO. She has also held numerous committee positions in these and other organizations. She convened the workshop leading to the ANSI/NISO thesaurus standard NISO Z39.19-2005, and was a member of the standards committee for its writing. She also acted as liaison to the British Standards Institute controlled vocabulary standards group to ensure that the U.S. and British standards would be compatible.

Margie is the founder and president of Access Innovations, Inc., which has been honored with many awards, including recognition several times by *KMWorld Magazine* as one of 100 Companies That Matter in Knowledge Management and as a Trend-Setting Product Company, as well as by *EContent Magazine* as one of 100 Companies That Matter Most in the Digital Content Industry. The company's information management services include thesaurus and taxonomy creation. Under Margie's guidance, Access Innovations has developed the Data Harmony® line of software for content creation, taxonomy management, and automated categorization for portals and data collections. The Data Harmony Suite is protected by two patents, numbers 6898586 and 8046212, and 21 patent claims. Her recognition of the value of automatic code suggestion for the medical industry led to the founding of Access Integrity and its Medical Claims Compliance system.

Margie's primary areas of research include automated indexing, thesaurus development, taxonomy creation, natural language processing, machine translations, and computer aided indexing. She has authored more than 200 published articles on these subjects. At industry and association meetings, she has given numerous workshops and presentations on thesaurus and taxonomy creation and maintenance.

Printed in the United States
by Baker & Taylor Publisher Services